THE HOLLYWOOD EPIC

Foster Hirsch

SOUTH BRUNSWICK AND NEW YORK: A. S. BARNES AND COMPANY
LONDON: THE TANTIVY PRESS

© 1978 by A. S. Barnes and Co., Inc.

A. S. Barnes and Co., Inc.
Cranbury, New Jersey 08512

The Tantivy Press
Magdalen House
136-148 Tooley Street
London SE1 2TT, England

Library of Congress Cataloging in Publication Data

Hirsch, Foster.
  The Hollywood epic.

  Bibliography: p.
  Filmography: p.
  Includes index.
    1. Historical films—History and criticism.
  2. Moving-pictures—United States. I. Title.
  PN1995.9.H5H57   791.43'7   77-82674
  ISBN 0-498-01747-8

PRINTED IN THE UNITED STATES OF AMERICA

Contents

Acknowledgments

Patrick Sheehan and Joe Balian at the Library of Congress; the staff of the
Library of Performing Arts, Lincoln Center, New York; the staff of the Film
Study Center at the Museum of Modern Art, New York; the libraries of
Brooklyn College and Columbia University; Bill O'Connell for photo research;
Peter Cowie; Ted Sennett; the library of the Academy of Motion Picture Arts
and Sciences; the Beverly Hills Public Library.

1. Historical Development

Epics are long narrative poems on grand subjects. Representative epics like *The Iliad, The Odyssey, The Aeneid, Beowulf, The Song of Roland,* and *The Cid* claim a hero who is a national leader, and involve an event—a battle, a journey, a quest—that is connected to the destiny of a nation. The epic hero is a saviour chosen by fate to represent his people. He is a transcendent character, though a human one, who is imperfect and struggling. He is a driven figure compelled by both external and internal forces to accomplish great deeds such as founding a country, leading his people to freedom, and protecting his king.

Epics are popularly conceived, action-filled stories that dramatise history and legend and that enforce elementary moral, religious, or political lessons. The epic is among the oldest of narrative forms, the earliest tales having been recited to primitive audiences by strolling minstrels who embroidered basic motifs with colorful new incidents. *The Iliad* and *The Odyssey* are thus culminations of a long oral tradition compounded of formulaic patterns in language, characterisation, and theme. Homer inherited a narrative that remained fluid despite the fact that it depended heavily on formulae. He codified the oral tradition by fixing it in language and by condensing its disparateness into a unified and artful narrative.

Homer's poems constitute the great epic of the ancient Greeks. The Old Testament is the great epic of the ancient Hebrews, and like Homer, it represents an accumulation of oral formulae—songs, poems, stories, myths, legends, and history—that are the remarkable literary heritage of a dispossessed people. The Old Testament recounts, in a variety of literary forms, the special covenant between the Hebrews and their God. It tells a monumental story of exile and return while at the centre of the epic canvas is the shifting relationship between a courageous, beleaguered people and their demanding, wrathful, vigilant God.

That these two essential epics—Homer and the Old Testament—were developed, piecemeal, over many generations, testifies to their national significance. The ancient Greeks and Hebrews regarded the stories contained in these great records as a precious national heritage; at the same time, therefore, that the stories were recited for purposes of entertainment, providing employment for the world's first actors, they also had strong connections to the political and religious life of the rapt audience. Homer's poems and the stories of the Old Testament express deep racial attitudes about fate and the nature of the cosmos; the stories, essentially simple in design, immediately accessible in theme, and already familiar to most of the listeners, satisfied basic needs both in terms of art and of national consciousness. The Homeric epics and the epic of the Old Testament had a magical appeal that endured for generations.

Epics are thus popular national ballads that celebrate heroic passages in the history of a people. Though they often contain moralistic and religious underpinnings, epics focus on action rather than philosophy; their stage is the public arena, and their hero is a man of affairs. The protagonists in these exciting sagas have little time for a tormented inner life, and therefore Moses rather than Hamlet qualifies as a quintessential epic hero.

Whether oral in origin, like Homer and the Old Testament, or literary, like Virgil, Milton, and Dante, the epic is defined by its vast scope (though, like *The Iliad*, its action might be confined to a brief time period) and its high theme. Epic action has a broad significance. Wars and battles, which often provide the central focus, are linked to national destiny. The epic can have a concentrated field of action (as in *The Iliad* or *The Song of Roland*)—a single crucial battle or encounter—or, more typically (as in *The Odyssey*), its structure can be episodic. Epics often use the free form *motif* of the journey in which many different incidents occur in a variety of settings.

With its broad movements through time and space, and its emphasis on action and external characterisation, the epic form is ideally suited to films. More fully than any other visual medium, films can accommodate the multiplicity and physicality of the traditional epic milieu. Literary epics, in fact, often anticipate films since they are filled with verbal equivalents of establishing shots and tracking shots: Homer ranges over columns of soldiers as they stand prepared for battle, and his war scenes are composed with calculated counterpoint between long shots and close-ups. Epics are intensely pictorial even when, as in the Old Testament, the poets do not allow themselves generous descriptions of setting or landscape. The cinema's fluid handling of space and time, its ability to depict physical reality and to render historical epochs concretely, and on a monumental scale, are ideal for the epic mode. Films offer visual equivalents for the verbal grandeur of literary epics. In artistic means, the epic is closer than any other literary form—the lyric, say, or the tragic—to the cinema. The vastness and scale that define the epic temper are capable of immediate realisation through film, and

yet epic material, which ought to qualify as a kind of pure cinema, has rarely enjoyed critical favor. Theorists and critics have traditionally attacked not only the often inferior execution of epic themes on film but the notion of the cinema's suitability to epic as well.

Hollywood epics, in particular, are customarily dismissed as garish vaudevillian spectacles, as sideshow attractions that trade on vulgarity and sensation while pretending to offer moral or religious uplift. The Hollywood epic has been condemned for its gaudiness, its overly elaborate decor and impoverished imagination, its earthbound assault on sublime themes, its presentation of history and legend in a mode that is contemporary and provincial. The Hollywood epic has been dismissed by auteur critics for denying directors the privileges of personal signature. Because of its size and cost and "importance," the epic has proven less congenial to directorial idiosyncrasy than other *genres* like the western, the musical, the thriller, the gangster film, and the domestic melodrama. Despite their formulaic tendencies, all of these other *genres* have proven elastic enough to accommodate the off-beat, high-strung styles of the most subversive of the Hollywood directors. Epic films must reach a wide audience in order to make a profit, and the huge budget serves as a restraint on originality. The epic is the most "official" of the Hollywood *genres*, and its critics claim that epic material demands a conservative approach, a flavourless high tone, a nobility that defeats innovation.

The high finance of epic film-making does necessarily limit a director. With the fate of a studio riding on his multi-million dollar project, he cannot afford to make an uncommercial *succès d'estime*, or a cult film coded with signs for the *aficionado*. The monumental film, like the classical epics of oral and literary tradition, must be immediately accessible to a broad popular audience.

Foreign directors engaged on epic subjects, however, have often enjoyed the freedom to experiment that American directors working for a major studio have rarely been able to claim. Directors like Fellini, Pasolini, Kurosawa, Leone, Lang, and Eisenstein have treated epic material in bold, original styles that would not be permitted in Hollywood.

The tyranny of the big studio front office has discouraged a radical approach to large-scale subject matter, and yet there have been many honourable, popularly conceived Hollywood epics; from

The Birth of a Nation in 1915 to *2001: a Space Odyssey* in 1968, a number of Hollywood-made films have attained the dignity and magnitude of the classical epic.

The standard Hollywood spectacle often displays visual amplitude and an elegant *mise en scène*, but even the most conscientious ones have problems with dialogue. Howard Hawks dismissed *Land of the Pharaohs* (1955) because he said he didn't know how pharaohs talked. Finding a convincing voice for ancient and historical characters is always a challenge for the film-maker. The poetry of the classical epics would be too difficult for language that is meant to be heard rather than read, and their inflated diction would sound particularly artificial within the physical reality that film establishes. Actors in realistic settings must sound real to a general audience. It is not surprising, therefore, that

epic films enjoyed their greatest critical acclaim in the silent period. The talking religious or historical blockbusters have seldom found a congenial diction, their dialogue remaining a stiff compromise between classical and contemporary rhythms. The epic movie still has to learn how to speak.

The two great epic cycles in Amercian films occurred during the silent period, from 1915 to 1927, and during the Fifties and early Sixties. In both periods, epics were produced as self-conscious demonstrations of the possibilities of film. Epic scope served as a display of cinematic virtuosity. D. W. Griffith's early films, culminating in the triumphs of *The Birth of a Nation* and *Intolerance* (1916), proved decisively that films were capable of handling grander subject matter than the theatre, and that the treatment of space and time, as well as of spectacle, was infinitely more elastic on film than

The greatest set in the history of movies: D. W. Griffith's monumental, fanciful version of ancient Babylon, for Intolerance, *1916.*

13

on stage. The early epics were primary means of confirming film's superiority over the theatre's strict physical limitations. It is significant that the first full-length film in the American repertory is *Judith of Bethulia* (1913), an epic subject; and that the first great American film, the one that established the new medium as an art form, was *The Birth of a Nation*.

With their action scenes and monumental *décor*, the earliest epic movies exploited the late Nineteenth-century theatrical vogue for spectacle. Theatregoers at the time were drawn to colossal production values; the naval battle and the chariot race in *Ben-Hur*, for instance, and the shopworn melodramas with spectacular last-minute rescues occurring in exotic locales, were particular favourites. The sensation melodramas that capitalised on audience interest in spectacle at the expense of story or characterisation clearly anticipated the ability of film to depict the "real world." These plays desperately sought to explode the restrictions of the proscenium by introducing realistically rendered scenes of action. But full-scale battles in the confines of the theatre can only seem like a stunt, no matter how splendid the production. Films could more naturally satisfy the contemporary infatuation with spectacle and thereby allow the theatre to return to small-scale dramas and comedies of intimate focus.

Films, then, rather than theatre, were the congenial medium for handling stories that depend on a vast time span, multiple settings, spectacle, and physical reality. And silent films were especially suitable for epic narratives, which traditionally contain a strong visual element and which emphasise action and movement rather than probing studies of character. Silence released the filmmakers from the need to create an epic language; stilted inter-titles were satisfactory for exposition and transition, and did not seriously interrupt the visual continuity. Silence conferred distance, and thereby insulated epic heroes from intimacy with the audience—silence allowed the larger-than-life characters to maintain their mythic stature. The emphasis on gesture and iconography in early epics universalised the action, so that Cecil B. DeMille's silent version of *King of Kings* (1927), for instance, has a timeless quality not attained by the sound film lives of Christ. DeMille's voiceless Christ is less particularised than the later, speaking impersonations, and the silence surrounds Christ with a suitably mystical aura. Silence gave symbolic force

to heroic gestures, while speech in period films has often restricted the scope of the action. Actors in epics often don't sound right, and flat dialogue and contemporary voices undercut the visual splendour. Since the words of epic figures like Moses and Christ are often formulaic and the main narrative lines are already familiar to most audiences, dialogue in epics based on traditional material can be an unnecessary duplication of the content conveyed by images.

Griffith and DeMille were the two major directors of silent epics, and they established many of the visual and thematic conventions of the *genre;* but there were films on epic themes that predated the work of these two pioneer filmmakers. J. Stuart Blackton made *The Life of Moses* in 1909. In both technique and content, it is a primitive film. The fixed camera, the painted backdrops, the rhetorical overacting, confine the action within a proscenium-like framework. Produced in the period before Griffith had begun to expand the grammar of film, Blackton's spectacle has the look of a filmed play; and a story filled with visual possibilities is reduced to a sequence of stilted *tableaux vivants*. The film has little visual interest, but even in this archaic rendition the story of Moses looks like a promising movie subject.

The main inspiration for epic films came from Italian spectacles rather than from native film and theatre sources. The Italian film industry had produced costume films as early as 1903, though these spectacles did not receive international attention until *Quo Vadis?* (1912) and *Cabiria* (1914) were released to wild acclaim. Griffith, a shrewd showman, and temperamentally drawn to spectacle, was impressed by the scale and length of these films (he had been trying unsuccessfully to persuade Biograph to allow him to make full-length pictures). Griffith was also impressed by the lavish way the Italian spectacles were presented in New York, with reserved seat, advanced-price performances scheduled twice a day. To compete with the Italian epics, Griffith designed *The Birth of a Nation* as a roadshow film, a major production to be presented with all the dignity and prestige of an important new play.

The Italian films were the first full-fledged movie epics; in length, production values, and thematic scope, they were more ambitious than anything American films had produced before the First World War. Italian culture has a consistent tradition of

The Little Colonel leading his men in battle, from one of the many precedent-setting war scenes in The Birth of a Nation, *1915, Hollywood's first major epic.*

operatic theatricality and grandeur, and this taste, along with the rich architectural heritage of Italian cities—classical buildings still standing and available for filming—made it inevitable that Italy would produce the first film spectacles. The epic tradition remains a part of the Italian sensibility, even as it is popularised and coarsened in latter-day "spear and sandle" sagas like *Hercules* and *Hercules Unchained*.

Despite their elaborate trappings, *Quo Vadis?* and *Cabiria* are rigid and, for the most part, unimaginative. Each scene consists basically of a single take, with the camera remaining in a stationary position at a neutral distance from the action. Moving at a plodding pace, the actors' gestures exaggerated and declamatory, the story lumbering along from one static set up to another, the films have none of the experimental daring, the fluidity, and the high-strung energy that mark Griffith's epics. But the films do have architectural sophistication, their sets an elaborate blend of historical reality and romantic fantasy.

Cabiria, set during the Punic Wars, is more accomplished than *Quo Vadis?* There is some attempt at camera movement, there is minimal intercutting within a scene to relieve visual monotony, and there are tentative efforts, through the use of close-ups, to establish audience identification with the characters. Cabiria, a Roman girl whose parents are killed in a volcanic explosion, is adopted by a Carthaginian princess, and saved by Roman spies Fulvius and his slave Maciste. Though there is an attempt to integrate the personal drama with the historical background, the film's narrative continuity is choppy. The director (Giovanni Pastrone)

15

Kirk Douglas entering the cave of the Cyclops in the Italian-made Ulysses, *1955, a poor relation to the great epic film tradition begun in Italy before World War I.*

and his screenwriters do not yet possess the visual vocabulary to cope with a panoramic canvas. The patriotic theme—Rome's victory over Carthage—is naïvely stated, and Cabiria, as a dramatic character, is extremely pale. But the character of Maciste, the Herculean slave who twice saves the tepid heroine, is thoroughly likeable (Maciste films continue to be a popular series in Italy). And the film contains generous amounts of spectacle, from the opening scene, in the snow, of Hannibal's army crossing the Alps; to the eruptive volcano; to the temple of Moloch, where children are sacrificed to a rapacious deity; to the climactic battle led by Scipio against the Carthaginians. The major scenes are treated like master paintings in which there is little movement within the frame. The big battle scene is statically filmed, from a single high angle long shot, and as a result it is ornamental rather than dramatic.

The set design has some wit and imagination, the temple of Moloch being shaped like the open mouth of a huge mythological beast supported by two menacing claws; and the princess's palace has ornate ceilings and marble floors with intricate mosaic patterns, and columns with an elephant *motif* that seems to anticipate the great Babylon set in *Intolerance*. A fantasia on African themes, the palace evinces a *horor vacui* that typifies contemporary taste for ornate clutter.

Inspired by the scale of the Italian epics, Griffith quickly surpassed them not only in scope but in style and substance as well. His five epic films—*Judith of Bethulia* (1913), *The Birth of a Nation* (1915), *Intolerance* (1916), *Orphans of the Storm* (1922), and *America* (1924)—constitute an unsurpassed achievement in the *genre*. Griffith's sensibility was that of a Southern gentleman with Victorian tastes in art and morals. Blatantly reactionary and sentimental, Griffith was a restless, instinctive artist whose experiments with cross-cutting, close-ups, camera

16

movement, and masking expanded the ability of film to manipulate space and time. Griffith developed the potential of film almost by accident, as practical solutions for narrating epic themes. For all their romantic *clichés* and philosophical soft-headedness, his epics have a visual energy that announced the arrival of a new art form.

DeMille's taste for the grandiose was as keen as Griffith's, but DeMille lacked Griffith's artistic integrity. It is DeMille's epics rather than Griffith's, however, that influenced the tone of the Hollywood blockbuster. To this day, "DeMille" is a kind of synonym for the Hollywood-style epic. Griffith's great films, like *The Birth of a Nation* and *Intolerance*, have a manic, obsessive quality, a deeply subjective colouring not traditionally part of the epic temper. DeMille's work is less idiosyncratic, less vigorous and demanding. Unlike Griffith, DeMille is not a mystic, not really even a romantic. His big films have a colder edge than Griffith's. Even at his best, in *King of Kings* or *The Ten Commandments* (1923 and 1956), DeMille's work lacks the imaginative sweep and the intense emtionalism of Griffith's films.

DeMille worked in three main subject areas: Biblical, American history, and sexy contemporary comedies with their trademark bathroom scenes. Tailored for mass appeal, all the DeMille films are the work of a master showman, as even the director's sternest critics admit. The films reflect an innately American sensibility in their eagerness to please, in their conspicuous extravagance, and in their inability to present another era except through a contemporary perspective.

Aristocratic decadence in Griffith's Orphans of the Storm, *1922, one of his five landmark contributions to the development of epic style on film.*

This stilted tableau from Orphans of the Storm *indicates Griffith's indebtedness to Nineteenth-century stage melodrama.*

DeMille always boasted of the accuracy of the historical reconstruction in his films (he employed huge research staffs), and yet his films, whether set in ancient Egypt or Rome or medieval Europe, always exude a robust though not altogether wholesome American quality, since there is usually a touch of the perverse in his standard sin and salvation sagas, a suggestion that sex is irresistibly appealing but morally unedifying. Mixing titillation with guilt, DeMille was seriously concerned with giving his audience a good show as well as enforcing a moral lesson. The sensibility underlying the films is thus both vaudevillian and puritanical. DeMille had grown up with the Bible in a pious household, and he thought of himself as a populariser of the Word of God.

For all his limitations, DeMille had the proper talents to produce successful epic films: an interest in spectacle for its own sake, a compulsion to entertain on a grand scale, and genuine convictions about religion and patriotism that provided a sturdy underpinning for his Biblical and historical extravaganzas. Some of his work, especially early silents like *Joan the Woman* (1917), *The Woman That God Forgot* (1917), the long prologue to the modern story in *The Ten Commandments*, and *King of Kings*, have more visual force and skill than critics have generally conceded. DeMille will never be taken seriously by serious critics since his films seldom transcend the level of *kitsch*; but in establishing the mold of the Hollywood epic, he was a vigorous, seminal pioneer.

Besides the work of Griffith and DeMille, the silent period produced major epics of various kinds: Biblical (*The Wanderer*, 1925; *Ben-Hur*, 1925; *Noah's Ark*, 1928); national (*The Iron Horse*, 1924;

The Exodus begins in DeMille's 1956 version of The Ten Commandments; *the destruction of the temple in DeMille's* Samson and Delilah, *1949. Hollywood's ultimate showman, DeMille was infatuated with ornate and towering ancient architecture.*

The Covered Wagon, 1923); Fairbanks swashbucklers like *Robin Hood* (1922) and *The Thief of Bagdad* (1924). Griffith and DeMille had rivals in their epic domain. Thomas Ince's *Civilization* (1916) was a self-conscious attempt to compete with *Intolerance* in fashioning a largescale morality drama. Ince's epic, like Griffith's, uses comparisons between widely separated historical epochs to underline a pacifist theme. J. Gordon Edwards, a secondrate director with a flair for gaudy spectacle, made several films in the teens with Theda Bara portraying temptresses of the ancient world. With their perfumed atmosphere, these films cultivated the vogue for the vamp. Edwards's taste was more lascivious and decadent than DeMille's—there was sex without moral uplift in his films—and Edwards pleased critics even less than DeMille did.

With the coming of sound, epic films were displaced in favor of other genres where sound and dialogue were more essential: comedies, gangster films, melodramas, and musicals dominated moviemaking for the next two decades. Wisecracks, repartee, the sounds of guns and of music shaped movie fantasies. The Thirties and Forties were the heyday of the major studio, and those films that could be made entirely on the back lot were preferred to those requiring location shooting, a necessity for most epics. During the Depression, audiences were drawn to light entertainment, to musicals and romantic comedies about people without money problems. And, on the other hand, they were enticed by gangster stories in which the protagonists challenged the system and, for a time, won. The gangster's meteoric rise to money and power contained a potent release for downtrodden moviegoers. Remote, stately epics, on the other hand, had little connection to the fantasy needs of Depression audiences. Sound films created the desire to hear colloquial American speech of the kind used at pell-mell pace by the gold-diggers, the con men, and the molls who populated contemporary *genre* movies. Sound films developed a rapid-fire style of delivery, a crackling, vigorous modern manner altogether foreign to the world of the epic.

DeMille continued his large-scale projects throughout the period. Films like *Cleopatra* (1934), *The Sign of the Cross* (1932), and *The Crusades* (1935) were given prestige bookings, though they seemed out of touch in a way that his silent epics had not. Costume films, high adventures, even standard epics, appeared sporadically throughout the Thir-

ties. The Errol Flynn swashbucklers at Warner Brothers, *Marie Antoinette* at Metro-Goldwyn-Mayer (1936), *The Last Days of Pompeii* (1935) at RKO, satisfied the diminished taste for spectacle. These films were made on a more modest scale than the silent epics, and they had little of the flair or the missionary spirit that typified the major silent spectacles. *Marie Antoinette* sentimentalised history by transforming the French queen into a high-minded heroine, a victim of mad revolutionaries. *The Last Days of Pompeii* fancifully rearranged history and theology by linking Christ to the apocalyptic explosion at Pompeii. The film tells the archetypal story of a gruff pagan who gradually converts to Christianity. It is a blunt, naïve morality drama that exalts faith over money, other-worldliness over materialism. The scenes of the eruption are truly impressive. Not part of any cycle or tradition, the film is situated in its period as a kind of lonely beacon, an oddity that had a popular success, thereby suggesting that the taste for a DeMille-like extravaganza that mixes visual thrills with a sermon is never entirely out of fashion.

Gone With the Wind, the most famous of all Hollywood epics, appeared at the end of the decade. It too was not a direct expression of its period; it isn't specifically a Thirties movie the way that *Little Caesar* or *The Gold Diggers* series or a Lubitsch high comedy are. *Gone With the Wind* has no direct contemporary relevance, and in this timeless, generalised quality, it is typical of the epic mode. Despite its unprecedented success, *Gone With the Wind* did not inaugurate an epic cycle since the taste of the Forties, like that of the Thirties, favored more modest *genre* films, ones that reflected in direct ways the moods of the country as it prepared for, fought in, and recovered from, the Second World War.

The emergence of the *film noir* in the Forties expressed the national mood of postwar disillusionment. Archetypal figures emerged during the period as manifestations of shifts in the national psyche. The most noticeable character types were those of strong, wilful women: the conniving spider woman who uses sex to get money; the matriarch who supplants the absent husband as breadwinner and head of the household; the defensive, desexualised career woman. The typical Forties melodrama had a heavier, more plodding texture than the light-fingered, quick-moving crime cycle of the Thirties. The later films suggest an atmosphere of universal corruption. In this milieu, epics were naturally

20

Fredric March disapproves of Roman decadence in The Sign of the Cross, *1932; Warren William and Claudette Colbert in* Cleopatra, *1934. Few epics were made in Hollywood in the 1930s, but DeMille almost single-handedly continued the tradition with lavish historical recreations like these two films.*

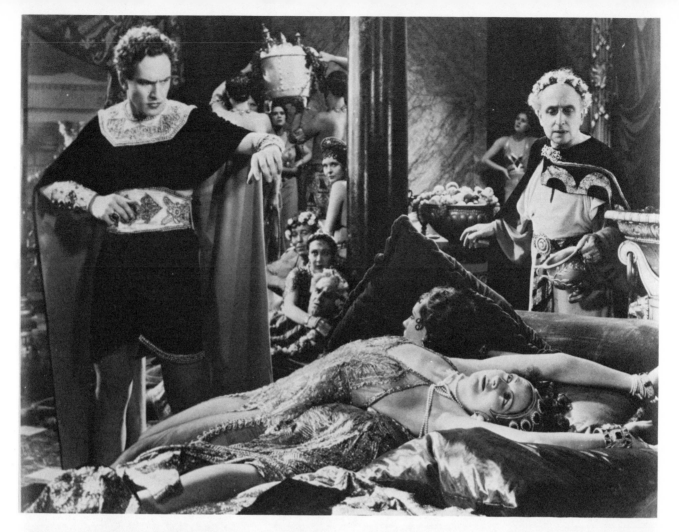

Clark Gable and Vivien Leigh, escaping from Atlanta, in Gone With the Wind, *1939, the most beloved of all Hollywood epics.*

displaced; and even David O. Selznick's *Duel in the Sun* (1945), his follow-up to *Gone with the Wind*, was a strained attempt at a sweeping epic style.

Late in the decade, in 1949, DeMille's *Samson and Delilah* revived an interest in spectacles. Lavish and mindless, DeMille's film was the precursor to the Golden Age of the Hollywood epic, the period that gathered momentum in the early Fifties and began to dwindle in the mid-Sixties.

This second epic phase in American films was prompted by a similar motive as the first: to prove that films were superior to a rival medium. This time, of course, the competition was television rather than the theatre; and the movies' defensive tactic of the wide screen (like silence) encouraged the production of epic subjects. In the early Fifties, when television became generally available, films lost a large segment of their audience. The studios

tried to lure people back to movies with the slogan that "movies are better than ever," though the phrase really meant that movies were *bigger* than ever. One large screen process after another—CinemaScope, VistaVision, Cinerama, Cinemiracle, Todd-AO—competed for the filmgoer's attention, and for the first time since its primitive history as a nickelodeon attraction, films sold themselves in a carnival atmosphere. At the same time that wide screens besieged the public, 3-D was launched; the idea was to startle, terrify, and unsettle audiences, to shake them up and give them a rousing show in ways that television could not. Moviegoers were assaulted as they had never been before. They were taken on a roller coaster ride; lions, horses, and arrows leapt out of the screen and onto their laps; and on the vast expanses of the oversized screens, big battles, panoramic landscapes, columns of slaves, and monumental architecture were paraded with great fanfare in order to impress audiences that movies were indeed more colossal than television.

The wide screen made certain aesthetic demands on the film-maker. Close-ups and rapid editing were not congenial to the CinemaScope frame. Wide screen composition required long shots, depth of field, and lengthy takes as opposed to Eisensteinian montage. The director had to compose his scenes with greater fluidity of movement within the frame since hectic cutting would be hard on the eyes.

Many purists were horrified by the wide screen, as they had been offended by the arrival of sound. To these critics, the large screen, like sound, represented a corruption of pure cinema, an artificial addition to the cinema's true and basic language. Other theorists felt that the wide screen increased the potential of film to capture objective reality. With its depth of field and its decreased emphasis on editing, the wide screen insured spatial and tem-

poral intergrity; the film-maker couldn't lie about space or time, couldn't rearrange objective reality into its most minute and therefore abstract components. The wide screen increased the possibilities for rendering the wholeness of physical reality and gave the viewer a greater share in the film by allowing him to select what he wanted to concentrate on in the frame. The introduction of the wide screen, then, revived the Eisenstein-Bazin dialectic: which method is more truly cinematic, the montage proposed by Eisenstein with its fragmented, manipulative presentation of reality, or the long takes and depth of field favoured by the neo-realists and celebrated by Bazin?

The wide screen was analogous to the arrival of sound in presenting technical hurdles for the film-maker. He had to overcome the threat of static compositions, and he had to learn to place actors

Hedy Lamarr and Victor Mature, in DeMille's Samson and Delilah, *1949, the film that revived Hollywood's interest in spectacular recreations of the ancient world.*

against settings and against each other in new ways. The wide screen director had to re-educate his own eye as he had to re-train the practised viewing habits of the audience. Movement within the frame, *mise en scène*, and lighting had to be re-interpreted for the elongated dimensions of the new screen.

Like most technical revolutions in film, the wide screen was greeted sceptically. It was considered a stunt that would not last, and the first films were regarded as bloated curiosities. Though wide screen films continue to be made (the process is now called Panavision), CinemaScope was partially defeated by television; concerned about movie sales to television, where wide screen films look uncomfortable, producers will often select the conventional ratio even for projects that seem to demand the larger frame.

Although it is not used as often as it should be, and seldom as creatively as it can be, the wide screen has survived, unlike Cinerama or 3-D. Cinerama was never fully explored as a medium for fiction films. Only a few non-travelogue films were made in the process, and only one, *2001: A Space Odyssey*, used the enormous curved screen with full creative intelligence. Other Cinerama films like *The Wonderful World of the Brothers Grimm, How the West Was Won, The Hallelujah Trail, Ice Station Zebra,* and *Krakatoa East of Java*, were sideshow curiosities that featured special effects. These movies had a circus quality, and producers, as well as audiences, began erroneously to assume that no good films could be made in Cinerama. 3-D was also short lived because it was used almost exclusively for exploitation films and the process (unfairly) earned a sleazy reputation.

The wide screen processes, which encouraged producers to make films on a spectacular scale that could not be duplicated on small home screens, naturally yielded an epic cycle. The first Cinema-Scope epic was *The Robe* (1953), chosen by 20th Century-Fox to showcase its new process because the religious subject seemed grand enough to fill the huge curved screen and because the project had the insurance of being based on Lloyd C. Douglas's phenomenally successful novel. The conservatively filmed story of religious conversion was wildly popular as both technical curiosity and high-powered drama. Its acceptance prompted a sequel, *Demetrius and the Gladiators* (1954), which was much less dignified (it was an epic potboiler), though it had a crude energy and the scenes of

gladiatorial combat used the wide screen in a more lively manner than the essentially static and ornamental parent film. Fox launched an epic cycle, beginning with another best-selling story set in the ancient world, Mika Waltari's *The Egyptian* (1954), and concluding, by the end of the decade, with threadbare films like *The Story of Ruth* (1960) and *Esther and the King* (1960), in which the epic scale had been significantly reduced.

Following the lead set by Fox, other studios plummaged the ancient world for stories with broad popular appeal. Metro-Goldwyn-Mayer produced *The Prodigal* (1955), *Ben-Hur* (1959), and *King of Kings* (1961); Warner Brothers presented *The Silver Chalice* (1954), *Land of the Pharaohs* (1955), and *Helen of Troy* (1956); Paramount offered *The Ten Commandments* (1956), Disney *The Big Fisherman* (1959), Columbia *Salome* (1953) and *Barabbas* (1961). Stories set in ancient Greece, Rome, Jerusalem, and Egypt, subjects taken from the Bible and screenplays based on slick best-selling novels with Biblical characters, became hot commercial properties. The story of Christ was especially popular, and any character or artifact (Barabbas, the silver chalice, the robe, the Big Fisherman) that touched on the life of Christ was grist for the epic mill. Each major studio had its own contender in the epic sweepstakes. Vehicles were manufactured in the grand manner for reigning movie queens, and hence the inappropriate displays of Rita Hayworth as Salome and Lana Turner as a pagan high priestess. The stars, as well as the directors, wanted to prove themselves in the epic revival.

Subjects other than those set in the ancient world were often given spectacular treatment—from stories on national themes like *Giant* (1956) and *Exodus* (1960), to inflated Westerns like *The Big County* 1958) and sprawling war films like *The Longest Day* (1962). Even films that were not epic in scale, like *Julius Caesar* (1953) and *Androcles and the Lion* (1953), had the look of the Fox Cinema-Scope extravaganzas. Grandiosity and elephantiasis attacked the industry.

Large-scale films continued to be made well into the Sixties; but inflated budgets, a tightened economy, and disappointing returns, eventually turned the major epic into a superannuated form. *Cleopatra* (1963) heralded the end of the phase. Its preposterous forty million dollar budget made epic films look like producers' folly, and with the commercial failure of late epics like *The Greatest Story*

Torin Thatcher and Richard Burton, in The Robe, *1953, the
first CinemaScope film. To show off the new wide screen process,
20th Century-Fox wisely chose an epic subject.*

Victor Mature and Michael Rennie, in Demetrius and the Gladiators, *1954, the quickly-made sequel to* The Robe.

Ever Told (1965) and *The Bible* (1966), it seemed clear that audience interest was elsewhere. The late Sixties' counterculture, the escalation of sex and violence in film, the wave of black exploitation films, all led to a demand for contemporary relevance that relegated the epics to the political and social blandness of the Fifties.

Except for isolated spectacles like those directed by Franklin Schaffner (*The Planet of the Apes*, 1968; *Patton*, 1970; *Nicholas and Alexandra*, 1971), epics were in disfavour from the mid-Sixties until recently, when film-makers like Francis Ford Coppola and Robert Altman began to redefine the uses of epic on film. In projects like *The Godfather* (1972, 1974) and *Nashville* (1975), Coppola and Altman use an epic format for themes and *milieux* not traditionally associated with the genre. Both films are modern-day epics with a sharp, contemporary

sensibility altogether different from the staid, impersonal canvases of conventional spectacles like *The Ten Commandments* and *Ben-Hur*.

Recently, too, some directors have worked on revisionist epics—Arthur Penn, *Little Big Man* (1970); Richard Lester, *Robin and Marian* (1976); Tony Richardson, *The Charge of the Light Brigade* (1967). By attacking the sanctity of war, by presenting American history from the point of view of the Indians, and by knocking legendary heroes off their pedestals, their films re-interpret epic and high romance in ways that formerly would have been considered subversive. Instead of simply inheriting it, films like these explore and question traditional epic subject matter. With their ironic spirit and their use of comedy and wit and contemporary references in solemn historic settings, they enlarge, while challenging, the possibilities of epic form and content on film.

After the Flood, in The Bible, *1966. Although it was intelligently done, the film was not a commercial success because by the mid-1960s popular interest in epics was nearly exhausted.*

Candice Bergen and Sean Connery, The Wind and the Lion, *1975, an echo of the great epic tradition in American films.*

It is unlikely that there will be a return to high Fifties epic, though from time to time, as isolated phenomena, there surely will be other films like John Milius's *The Wind and the Lion* (1975), which recalls the virtues of the traditional Hollywood epic in celebrating heroism and in treating the audience to a feast of stunningly photographed landscapes. The film, a parade of conventionally composed long shots of intense sunsets and of riders silhouetted against vast horizons, is cinema's equivalent to purple prose, and a salute to the great Hollywood epic tradition.

Columbia's Salome, *1953 with Rita Hayworth; Warner Brothers'* Helen of Troy, *1955, with Jacques Sernas as Paris. Each major studio had at least one entry in the 1950s epic sweepstakes.*

2. Aspects of Style

The Hollywood epic presents a conservative view of the ancient world. Its sense of the past is based on visual conventions borrowed from Victorian paintings, Nineteenth-century stage design, the *décor* in the early Italian epics and in the pioneering work of Griffith and DeMille. The presentation of ancient splendour varies little in the Hollywood extravaganza; ancient Rome or Jerusalem looks much the same in the Fifties as it did in the Twenties. Hollywood's standardized conception of epic backgrounds was a function of economics; a big budget film cannot risk challenging popular preconceptions with eccentric, revisionist visual depictions of the ancient world as savage or dangerous or truly alien. A multimillion dollar spectacle cannot afford to offer a radical, daring re-creation of the past. Hence, the epic, like other movie genres, relies on visual clichés that have been developed through repetition and are based on audience familiarity. Experienced moviegoers know what ancient Rome or Greece or Egypt is supposed to look like, and any film that seriously counters these received notions is not likely to gain popular acceptance.

Griffith and DeMille instructed audiences as well as other film-makers in how to perceive the ancient world. Though few American films since *Intolerance* have been planned on such a monumental scale, few have substantially differed in their view of the past.

Griffith's Babylon is the prototype for Hollywood's standard re-creation of ancient splendour and decadence. With its towering walls, its broad ramparts, its immense, heavily ornamented gate, its thick, fluted columns, and its fanciful elephant *motif,* the Babylon set is unsurpassed in size and impact; it has become, quite properly, the unofficial symbol of Early Hollywood. And its lounging monarchs swathed in silks and brocades and surrounded by palm trees, dancing girls, leopards, and acres of food, are ultimate depictions of Mediterranean luxury. The heroine of the Babylon episode, a coy mountain girl with a crush on the King, introduces a distinctly contemporary note in the visual grandeur; she is a way of connecting the background magnificence to the moviegoer because her presence suggests that, after all, the ancients were fundamentally no different from us. Griffith, then, established epic precedent in both the magnitude of his set and the contemporaneity of his main character. Participants in most Hollywood epics conduct their affairs in luxurious settings while acting, thinking, looking, and (later, after 1927) talking like Twentieth-century Americans.

Hollywood's view of the past is based on historical reality that is nevertheless heavily glamorised. Griffith and DeMille insisted on the accuracy of details in costuming and architecture while enter-

29

Hollywood's typical rendition of ancient splendor: Metro's mammoth Roman Forum built for Quo Vadis?, *1952.*

taining fanciful distortions of historical fact. Intertitles in *Intolerance* and *The Birth of a Nation* proudly announce that big set pieces like the towers of Babylon and Ford's Theatre, where Lincoln was assassinated, are exact historical facsimiles. Publicity for the DeMille extravaganzas emphasised the director's battery of research assistants and the years of background work that insured a historically correct re-creation of the past. But the immaculate temples, forecourts, arenas, and marketplaces of the epic milieu, the burnished gold, the marble, the rich silks and draperies, look inescapably like opulent movie fantasies rather than a faithful depiction of ancient reality. The gleaming beauty of the sets, with their rigorous denial of dirt, suggests a conspiratorial revision of historical truth: the typical *mise en scéne* of the Hollywood epic is too elaborate

The mountain girl (Constance Talmadge), in "The Fall of Babylon" episode from Intolerance. *Her lively contemporary personality offset the grandeur of the sets and encouraged audience identification.*

and symmetrical to pass as a reflection of even a remote objective reality, and so the directors' claims of authenticity are beside the point. It isn't the literal visual truth of the ancient world that audiences are interested in anyway, but *kitsch* fantasies of pomp and luxury.

Hollywood's predilection for the grandiose was anticipated by the late Nineteenth-century academic paintings of classical scenes by artists like John Martin, Alma-Tadema, Gérome, and Bougoureau, who cleaned up history and overlaid it with a Victorian infatuation for fussy detail. The ancient world as conceived by these Nineteenth-century artists is incredibly lavish—far grander, probably, than the original. Their huge, crowded, bursting canvases have the overstuffed quality of a Victorian interior. Griffith and DeMille were famil-

iar with the work of these painters, who enjoyed an enormous vogue at the time the two directors first began planning their epic films.

The academic paintings, like the epic film itself, are an index of taste that has passed; both have a stately, ornate quality that seems hopelessly square to modern sensibilities. Preoccupied with elaborately detailed spectacle, academic paintings, like Victorian sensation melodrama, strained to shatter the circumference of their frames and to expand the visual possibilities of their medium. With their multiple settings and feverish cross-cutting, the theatrical spectacles anticipated the plastic qualities of film, while the bloated Victorian paintings, with their often exaggerated angles, extreme long shots, and hectic activity, seemed to cry out for movement.

Playing a high priestess in Old Testament Jerusalem, in The Prodigal, *1955, Lana Turner looks unmistakably like a star of the 1950s.*

Make-up and costume in the typical epic are often adjusted to the period when the film was made, so that, in 1934, beneath the spangles and elaborate headdresses, Claudette Colbert's Cleopatra looks like a contemporary party girl, while Elizabeth Taylor's 1963 Cleopatra has visual reminiscences of Sixties chic. Playing a high priestess in Old Testament Jerusalem in *The Prodigal*, Lana Turner sports the hair-do and the tailoring of a well-turned-out star of the Fifties. The concessions to period in spectacle films, particularly noticeable in the wardrobe of the leading ladies, resemble the contemporary touches given to religious paintings in which Christ appears in Renaissance garb, for instance, or delivers the Sermon on the Mount in a neo-classic landscape, with ruined temples and palaces as incongruous backdrops. Protecting star image with echoes of modern dress represents the power of the star performer to re-shape and sometimes to defeat history; and the procession in epic films of decidedly contemporary-looking actresses like Lana Turner and Rita Hayworth and Joan Collins points up Hollywood's essentially glamorised and cleaned-up treatment of the past.

The sets in Hollywood epics compete for size and grandeur but seldom for originality. The big sets are always the same: the arena, the gates of the city, the senate chamber, the throne room; and they are practically interchangeable in their pristine marble elegence, their symmetry, their intricately patterned walls and ceilings and floors. Griffith's Babylon; DeMille's towering gates and symmetrical double row of statues for the Egyptian city of Per-Ramses in both versions of *The Ten Commandments*; the Colosseum in *Ben-Hur, Quo Vadis?* (1951), and *Barabbas*; the Roman Forum in *The Fall of the Roman Empire* (1964); the harbour, marketplace, and temples of Alexandria in *Cleopatra* (1963) are all designed on a colossal scale with the intent of being stupendous and breathtaking.

Each studio offered its own variations on the standard epic scenery. Fox sets, for example, tended to be solid and squat, whereas Metro-Goldwyn-Mayer's spectacles had a glossier, more evanescent texture. Musicals could be set in the Metro *décor*, while that would be unthinkable amid the Fox heaviness. But on the whole, the elaborate backgrounds show little change from film to film and from decade to decade; like the standard temple exterior for Greek tragedy, the Hollywood vision of ancient *décor* is immutable in its remote beauty and its imperviousness to human drama.

The epic films' visual treatment of recurrent character types—infidels and believers, pagans and Christians—is also conventional. The faithless are traditionally associated with luxurious dissipation and they are typically observed at sensual bashes conducted in the banquet hall or the arena. The scenes of pagan revelry are overloaded, as in *Intolerance*; the frame is filled with swirling activity, with (in later films) splashes of reds and purples, whereas for the religious characters and for the moments of spiritual illumination, the design is spare, usually depending on stark chiaroscuro lighting or on tones of grey and white.

The Hollywood epic, then, depicts the ancient world in traditional ways, through a set of visual conventions inherited from Victorian paintings and stage design, and from the early Italian epics and those of Griffith and DeMille. There are, however, occasional modulations of visual stereotype, usually in the direction of either greater opulence or greater austerity. Sets and the use of colour for *David and Bathsheba* (1951), *Solomon and Sheba* (1959), and *The Greatest Story Ever Told* are, for instance, noticeably subdued. The bare grey palaces in these films look as if they belong in an ancient desert kingdom. The films' plain, even severe, architectural design shifts the emphasis from background ornamentation to foreground drama.

The underrated *Barabbas* also reworks visual convention in the handling of Biblical themes. The Crucifixion scene was photographed during an actual eclipse of the sun, and the resulting half-light provides a brooding, mystical quality. In *King of Kings*, Nicholas Ray pierces convention by regrouping the disciples at The Last Supper, and by shooting part of the scene from a startling high angle that explodes the traditional perspective of the Da Vinci painting. Salome's dance in *The Greatest Story Ever Told* challenges the usual staging of bacchanals in Biblical films by its absolute simplicity. The huge throne room is empty as Salome dances, her movements picked out by isolated pools of light. The *mise en scène* has a sinister quality that intensifies the drama. *The Big Fisherman* contains another fresh treatment of pagan revelry as the movement of celebrants is seen through a transparent curtain, their actions outlined as ominous shadows.

The long opening section in *The Fall of the Roman Empire* offers another kind of visual surprise. Marcus Aurelius's wooden fortress, set in a snow-bound mountain forest, looks wonderfully unfamiliar, its wood-lined rooms serving as a novel

Hollywood monumentality: The Colosseum in Ben-Hur, *1959;*
the Roman Forum in The Fall of the Roman Empire, *1964.*

33

Two impressionistic sets from The Silver Chalice *(with Jack Palance), 1954, Hollywood's most visually experimental treatment of ancient architecture.*

kind of epic backdrop. The film is strikingly designed throughout, and the Forum competes with Griffith's Babylonian forecourt and the Colosseum in *Ben-Hur* (1925 and 1959) as one of the great movie sets. The film showers the viewer with a dazzling reconstruction of classical architecture, the exteriors an array of pristine facades, the palace interiors a riot of colours, of intricate mosaic patterns, of columns and arches. The exuberant sets overwhelm the weak story and mostly indifferent performances. Produced near the end of the epic cycle by Samuel Bronston, the last of the big-time Hollywood spenders, *The Fall of the Roman Empire* looks like the final gasp of Old Hollywood extravagance. The film's *décor* displays a luxuriance and scale that could not be duplicated in today's economy, and that already seemed anomalous in 1963.

The Silver Chalice, though, is the most visually

34

This stately tableau from The Ten Commandments *(with Charlton Heston, Yvonne de Carlo, John Derek, Debra Paget, and Nina Foch) is typical of DeMille's conservative* mise en scène. *The great showman reserved a visually exuberant style for his big set pieces, such as the earthquake from his original version of* The Ten Commandments.

experimental Hollywood epic. Repelled by the script, and generally disrespectful of the *genre* anyway, critics didn't give proper recognition to the film's daring use of simplified, non-representational *motifs*. The film's rendering of ancient Rome and Jerusalem is a blend of the semi-abstract and the impressionistic. Its sense of ancient architecture is fanciful yet informed, and the film is enhanced by its delicate use of colour and its strong contrasts between black and white. Based on a bloated novel by Thomas B. Costain, the film is flatfooted in its treatment of story and characters, but beguiling in its decor.

The Silver Chalice is rivalled only by William Cameron Menzies's famous sets for Douglas Fairbanks's *The Thief of Bagdad*. The design for both films has a free-wheeling, imaginative flavour that is rare in big-budget American films. Perhaps because *The Thief of Bagdad* was clearly romantic fantasy rather than epic, the studio permitted the dazzling, free-form style of Menzies's concepts. The towers and minarets of Menzies's fanciful Bagdad soar over the characters while matching Fairbanks's buoyancy. The sets are grand yet lightweight, enclosing the actors in a sprightly holiday atmosphere. The film's lyrical design avoids completely the weighty, baroque ornamentation that is standard for epic subjects.

Heavily conventionalised, the epic style as adapted by the Hollywood studios discouraged the creation of the personal epic. Directors of spectacles had to conform to the dictates of the worried front office, anxious to protect its investment and therefore insisting on caution and restraint. *The Birth of a Nation* and *Intolerance* are the two great personal epics in American films, and Griffith never managed entirely to recover from the financial failure of the latter. Significantly, it was DeMille who set the predominant epic style. DeMille, a conservative stylist, uses the camera, for the most part, as a neutral recording instrument objectively observing a sequence of spectacular events. DeMille's *mise en scène* is stately and processional, avoiding modern techniques like the jump cut, the zoom, or the restlessly moving camera. DeMille's camera is in fact often stationary for intimate scenes, with nothing more than conventional reverse angle editing for variety and emphasis. The pyrotechnics are reserved for the set pieces like the exodus, the parting of the Red Sea, the bacchanal at the Golden Calf. For these moments of sideshow spectacle,

DeMille uses a more aggressive technique, with much intercutting and with extreme high angle shots that proudly display the vast sets and the hordes of extras. Relying on a traditional style essentially unchanged from his work in silent films, DeMille is never self-conscious in his use of film form. He maintained an aloofness from his vast subjects that paralleled the detachment of the ancient epic storytellers and that set the norm for the impersonal style of the typical Hollywood spectacle.

Ponderous in theme and *décor,* made over a long span of time at enormous costs and with many assistants, epics cannot accommodate directorial eccentricity as readily as less pretentious *genres.* Nicholas Ray's *Party Girl* is more expressive, more personal, than his work on *King of Kings* or *55 Days at Peking* (1963); Robert Rossen's *Lilith* and *The Hustler* are more individual films than his *Alexander the Great* (1956); *Spartacus* (1960) is Stanley Kubrick's least engaged project. These epic films signed by directors often heralded for their distinctive styles are less flavourful, less neurotic and obsessive, than their work in other *genres*; but the large-scale films provided the directors different kinds of visual challenges. *Spartacus*, in particular, is expertly made, with many elegantly composed shots and a powerfully rendered atmosphere of aristocratic decadence. Regardless of Hollywood's conservative visual concept of the past, regardless of the imaginative restrictions placed on the director, the epic format offers many opportunities for virtuoso cinema.

Almost all Hollywood epics can claim moments of startling beauty and impact. The requisite scenes—battles, balls, banquets, ceremonial processions, combat in the arena—are usually skillfully filmed. In both successful and flawed epics, it is the big set pieces (which correspond to set speeches in classical drama, for which the audience is primed) that people remember. In these charged moments, money and craft are aggressively on display; and at the same time that we are expected to participate in the excitement of the scene, as a climactic moment in the dramatic action, we are also encouraged to see the grand moments in a kind of double focus, as a fantastic expenditure of money and ingenuity. How did they ever do it? and How much did it cost? are questions that run through the audience's mind. The high points in Hollywood epics become, as Michael Wood has noted in *America in the Movies*, something of a metaphor for American ambition, vulgarity, and worship of materialism—these set pieces are a maximum display of every dollar invested.

The big moments in epics supply a catalogue of Hollywood as its gaudiest, its most expansive, its most eager to please. Epics have given movies some of their grandest visual statements; epic subjects have provided directors with opportunities for extravagant compositions, from the victory celebration in *Intolerance,* to the wagon train snaking through the desert in *The Covered Wagon,* to the exodus in *The Ten Commandments,* to the chariot race in *Ben-Hur,* to Cleopatra's entry into Rome. Epic themes are crystallised in spectacular public activity, in balls and processions and battles that demand the movement and scale possible only through film. The epic subject is a summons for the long shot, the high-angle overhead shot, the tracking, craning camera; for deep focus, Griffith cross-cutting, and Eisenstenian montage; for, in short, a full range of film grammar.

Epics have bequeathed to film history a gallery of exciting climaxes, scenes of massive movement and cataclysmic upheaval: the battles in *The Birth of a Nation;* the flood in *Noah's Ark;* the rush to claim land in *Cimarron* (1931); the volcanic eruption in *The Last Days of Pompeii;* the burning of Atlanta in *Gone With the Wind;* the destruction of the temple in *Samson and Delilah,* in *The Prodigal,* and again in *Solomon and Sheba;* the parting of the Red Sea in *The Ten Commandments;* the retreat of Napoleon's army in *War and Peace* (1956); the prison break in *Exodus;* the revolt of the slaves in *Spartacus;* the attack on a desert fortress in *Lawrence of Arbaia* (1962). Many isolated images in epic films indicate the grandiose scale on which the films are conceived: the Victorian mansion, in splendid solitude on the sprawling Texas ranch, in *Giant;* Patton, a miniature figure in front of a gigantic American flag; a line of soldiers silhouetted against the horizon in *Cheyenne Autumn* (1964), or *The Searchers* (1956),

One of the many memorable visual set pieces in epic films: the wagon train crossing the river in The Covered Wagon, *1923.*

Visual set pieces: the chariot race in Ben-Hur, *1959; marching
to battle in the Russian* War and Peace, *1964–1967.*

Visual set piece: the burning of Rome in Quo Vadis?, *1951*.

Set pieces: the revolt of the slaves in Spartacus, *1960; the attack on the desert fortress in* Lawrence of Arabia, *1962.*

or *Stagecoach* (1939); the slain El Cid, photographed from a low angle, propped upon his horse, the sun glinting brilliantly off his shield; Tara looming proudly over the landscape in *Gone With the Wind*.

When an epic succeeds, the spectacle is organically connected to the human drama, and the films earn their florid set pieces. The two most elaborate big scenes in American films, the exodus in *The Ten Commandments* and the chariot race in *Ben-Hur*, are logically connected to the stories that surround them. The films have been realised on a scale that supports these aggressive displays of Hollywood know-how and showmanship. When, on the other hand, the intended epic fails in its treatment of a large-scale subject, it seems to have been made solely for its sensational elements. *How the West Was Won* (1962) fails as an epic statement of a national theme because it is, in effect, nothing more than a collection of spectacular scenes. A pioneer

The ancestral house as epic image: Tara, in Gone With the
Wind; *the isolated Victorian mansion,* in Giant, *1956.*

The buffalo stampede, one of a series of spectacular climaxes, in How the West Was Won, *1962.*

family's fight with a rampaging river, a buffalo stampede, and a showdown on a train are designed to take advantage of the Cinerama screen; they are moments of high excitement that the audience has been waiting for as a release from the lacklustre story and trite characters. It is the same sort of "arrangement" that audiences have with the recent phenomenon of the disaster epic, where viewers agree to sit through the dull stories of *Earthquake* and *The Towering Inferno* in anticipation of a rousing finale that showcases the latest gimmicks in Hollywood technology.

In many epics that only partially succeed, however, there are moments where the director amplifies his large subject with striking visual concepts. There is a stunning scene in Mervyn Leroy's middling *Quo Vadis?*, for instance, when the camera, placed at an extreme angle, peers down on thousands of rebelling Romans rushing forward to dismantle Nero's palace. The scene has a sense of urgency and magnitude that most of the film lacks. Howard Hawks makes skilful use of the wide screen in *Land of the Pharaohs,* especially in his documentary-like sequence of the building of the pyramids where he arranges his hordes of extras in linear groupings to emphasise the breadth of the frame. Unlike Eisenstein, who fragments time and space in *Battleship Potemkin* (1925) or *Ten Days That Shook the World* (1928), Hawks uses a minimum of cutting and instead favors long takes and a gracefully roving camera that preserve spatial integrity. *Land of the Pharaohs* is not a fully satisfying film because the story is no match for Hawks's visual elegance in the opening procession of Pharaoh returning in triumph to his city, and in the intricately patterned, deep focus shots of the construction of the pyramid. But the director's use of the wide screen has an epic grandeur that, at times, transcends the uninspired screenplay.

Similarly, King Vidor's mostly foolish treatment of *Solomon and Sheba* yet contains a vigorously presented battle scene replete with striking tracking shots of rows of foot soldiers and extreme long shots that stress the vast number of warriors. The trick that Solomon's army uses against the enemy—their shields reflect the sun and blind their opponents—provides a splendid visual moment. Anthony Mann's lacklustre *55 Days at Peking* has a rousing prologue that promises more than the film delivers: in a practically unbroken series of expressive movements, the camera tracks and cranes from one foreign section of the besieged city to another. This opening vividly and compactly defines the film's setting and heightens audience expectation.

In Hollywood epics, the word has seldom proven equal to the image, which is why silent films found epic subjects congenial. Characters in silents are icons and masks; silence emphasises external qualities and invests gestures with universal sig-

Skillful wide screen composition, with deep focus and horizontality, in Howard Hawks's Land of the Pharaohs, *1955.*

King Vidor's beautifully designed battle scene, in Solomon and Sheba, *1959. Yul Brynner as the warrior king.*

43

The city as epic image: Samuel Bronston's large-scale recreation of Peking for 55 Days at Peking, *1963*.

nificance. Speech restricts characters and demands a naturalistic style of performance, whereas epic heroes embody precisely those generalised, external, mythic qualities immediately available to the silent screen actor. Monumental performances in silent epics have never been duplicated in sound films. Lillian Gish in *Orphans of the Storm* raises melodrama to epic through her operatic emotionalism; Falconetti suggests spiritual transcendence in Dreyer's *The Passion of Joan of Arc* (1928)—her acting has an emotional grandeur that could only be contained and diminished by the addition of dialogue. H. B. Warner's Christ in *King of Kings* is a radiant figure, and it is unlikely that a Christ who speaks could be as powerful an icon.

Psychological complexity and the examination of feelings are not, of course, inaccessible to silent films; but, for epic subjects, in which texture and surface are crucial, speech introduces a realistic dimension that mars the abstract, distanced epic framework. As in Homer, sight rather than sound is often sufficient for the communication of the epic theme. Sound films, an amalgam of image and word, have always found it difficult to forge a verbal style appropriate to the epic background. Characters in settings that look real cannot speak in an inflated literary style without incurring disbelief; the heightened, artificial, and often formulaic language of the literary epic cannot work comfortably within the concrete physical reality established by films. Hollywood screenwriters, however, have seldom discovered how to make epic heroes speak in a manner at once real and yet properly elevated; for dignity, the writers are often content simply to omit contractions. Efforts to be hip, to deny the problem of historical verisimilitude by brazenly flaunting it, as in Anthony Harvey's *The Lion in Winter* (1968) and, in places, Joseph L. Mankiewicz's *Cleopatra*,

44

have reduced historical figures to smart-talking contemporaries. The method has its charm, but it is suitable mostly for comic dissonance that mocks epic characterisation and theme. The usual compromise is to settle for a bland diction that is a mixture of the high-flown and the down-to-earth. This approach can be counted on to produce some unintentionally comic lines. DeMille's sound epics are a particularly rich source of howlers; in *The Ten Commandments*, a very modern-sounding Anne Baxter croons to Charlton Heston, "Oh Moses, Moses, you splendid, stubborn, adorable fool!"

Characters in epic are thus observed as icons seen typically in long shot rather than close-up; they are larger-than-life figures who participate in ceremonies and who create legends. For this reason, the epic style has little use for the ability that most film actors have to behave in lifelike ways. Most American movie stars become successful because they

embody an average yet idealised manner that popular audiences can identify with; but epic films cannot use this relaxed kind of "behaving" that frequently passes for acting, since epic subjects demand distance from the commonplace and the daily. Epic roles require a heightened, anti-naturalistic style that presupposes some classical training. Hence, theatre-trained English actors, with experience in the classical repertory, sound appropriate in togas and robes, whereas the more plain-spoken American actor is too conspicuously contemporary. In costume pictures, set in the ancient world, there are few distinguished performances from American stars. Clark Gable is totally convincing as Rhett Butler, but as an ancient Roman, a medieval King, or a questing knight, he would have been preposterous. Laurence Olivier's Henry V is one of the great portraits of an epic hero in films; but what American film star is capable of

Charlton Heston, in El Cid, *1961: Characters in epics, who participate in ceremonies and who create legends, are seen typically in long shot rather than close-up.*

the kind of rhetorical styling the part demands? Richard Burton, Peter O'Toole, John Gielgud, Robert Morley, Finlay Currie, Deborah Kerr, and Jean Simmons have all been believable in period pieces, while Lana Turner, Rita Hayworth, Claudette Colbert, and Robert Taylor have not. Robert Taylor as Ivanhoe or as Marcus in *Quo Vadis?* has the sturdy, energetic look that befits an epic hero, but whenever he speaks in his flat mid-American drawl, cinematic illusion collapses. Charlton Heston is the one American actor with a creditable record of epic characterisations. Grim, squarejawed, oversized, he has the proper iconographic qualities for Moses or Ben-Hur (and he is excellent in both parts); his granitic presence, his orotund voice, and his oratorical delivery complement the traditional visual style of Hollywood epics.

3. Foreign Epics

The results of the Hollywood style adapted to epic themes are often grandiose and visually striking; but the studio system that financed the films stifled a personal, revisionist approach to massive subjects. Significantly, there was no place in Hollywood for Eisenstein, perhaps the greatest of epic directors in film. In some ways, Hollywood's conventional approach to epic themes conformed to the characteristics of classical oral and literary epics since *The Aeneid, Beowulf, The Song of Roland,* and *The Cid* are official poetry that depends on formulaic *motifs* and a generalised, impersonal tone; the epic writer or bard celebrates his subject rather than himself, and his use of language is less particular, less self-glorifying, than that of the Romantic or the contemporary *avant-garde* poet. The anonymous writer of classical epic did not in fact strive for an original or startling voice; he was content to record great events in language that was vigorous, often splendid, but not remarkable for its individual qualities of tone or structure.

Though the epic is the most official and communal of literary *genres,* it is not of course immune to a radical voice. But the studio's huge investments in spectacles curtailed opportunities for experiment, and most of the daring variations of epic style are to be found in the work of non-American directors who were not chained by big studio insecurity.

In the silent period, the work of Eisenstein in Russia and of Fritz Lang in Germany offered significant alternatives to the American epics being produced by Griffith, Ince, J. Gordon Edwards, and DeMille. Eisenstein has written of his great admiration of Griffith; and *Intolerance*, in fact, was the central "text" at the Russian Film School run by Pudovkin. Eisenstein appreciated especially Griffith's refinement of cross-cutting, which allowed for the presentation of simultaneous events occurring in different locales. But Eisenstein felt that Griffith did not fully exploit this powerful piece of film punctuation; and he criticized the American director for confining parallel editing to the melodramatic last-minute rescue as opposed to using it to enforce an ideological point. Griffith, in short, was not a political thinker, not an abstract theorist in the way Eisenstein was; he was a Romantic.

But for all his self-conscious theorising about film form, Eisenstein was as impassioned as the sentimental, intuitive Griffith in his approach to epic subjects. Like Griffith, Eisenstein used epic format as a kind of propaganda, and *Battleship Potemkin* and *Ten Days That Shook the World* were made to celebrate the Revolution just as *The Birth of a Nation* was made to correct Northern assumptions about Reconstruction and *Intolerance* was presented in order to endorse a pacifist, humanitarian point of view.

Eisenstein's montage theory, based on a series of

unrelenting visual conflicts, of dialectical collision within and between shots, was a useful device for epic material, but it was too formally self-conscious, too demanding and intense, to be widely applicable to Hollywood films. In *Potemkin*, Eisenstein rarely allows the audience to relax as he showers it with a series of conflicts in graphics, volume, direction of movement, and length of shots. Eisenstein splinters action and time into almost abstract fragments; his method allows the director great freedom in rearranging reality and in underscoring the significance of individual actions and events. Eisenstein's frantic, dynamic editing is especially suited for depicting scenes of battle and chaos. The famed Odessa Steps sequence from *Potemkin*, with its contrast between film time and real time, its explosion of the action into fragmented units, its insistent conflict between the linear, methodical movement of the Tsarist soldiers and the chaotic actions of the fleeing civilians, is a spectacular showcase for montage.

The battle on the ice in Eisenstein's *Alexander Nevsky* (1938) is also eloquent testimony to the power of dynamic cutting. With its symmetrical arrangement of soldiers against the horizon, its stark contrasts between the black costumes of the warriors and the glaring whiteness of the snow, its counterpoint between the images and Prokofiev's bursting music, the long sequence has the aura of an intensely stylised ritual.

Rooted in objective reality, Eisenstein's vision is nonetheless too rhetorical and self-intoxicated to have achieved a wide influence on American epics. Yet many directors engaged in epic projects have closely studied the Odessa Steps and battle on the ice sequences; and many of the memorable battle scenes in film history, from Olivier's *Henry V* (1944) to Michael Curtiz's *Charge of the Light Brigade* (1936) to Kubrick's *Spartacus* to Sergei Bondarchuk's *War and Peace* (1964-67), with their rapid, propulsive editing, their startling conflicts between long shot and close-up, and among horizontal, vertical, and diagonal patterns of movement, are indebted to Eisenstein's experiments.

For all its usefulness as a model for the visual choreography of action scenes, *Potemkin* could not have been made in Hollywood because it presents the mass, rather than the individual, as hero, and because its unrelenting visual dynamics are too self-conscious to be accepted by a wide popular audience. *Potemkin* is the kind of self-regarding movie that Hollywood has traditionally distrusted.

After a lengthy period of exile, Eisenstein returned to turbulent events in Russian history with his production of *Ivan the Terrible* (Part I, 1943; Part II, 1946). He developed for his two-part film a different kind of epic style from the dazzling rhythms and textures of *Potemkin*. Extravagantly slow-moving, *Ivan the Terrible* stresses continuity between shots rather than collision and dissonance. The film is preoccupied with architectural symmetry; the actors, enclosed by arches and columns, are arranged formally within the frame. Individual shots are longer and more densely composed than in *Potemkin*. Low angle shots are used expressively to emphasise Ivan's stature and to distort the faces of his opponents. In *Potemkin*, Eisenstein fragmented time and space, and accelerated the action, in order to heighten the symbolic import of events; here, he uses stasis to inflate the action to epic proportions.

N. Cherkassov's operatic rendition of Ivan (inconceivable in an American film because it is so baroque, so giddily detached from reality) is one of the great epic performances in film. With its deliberate, expansive gestures, its prolongation of dramatic moments, its pictorial posturing, its sepulchral, incantatory verbal rhythms, Cherkassov's is a rare kind of heroic acting. It has a touch of absurdity—it is, after all, so self-infatuated; but it is an exhilarating display of theatrical technique. Cherkassov is as extroverted as Falconetti in Dreyer's *Passion of Joan of Arc* is introverted, and both dangerously extreme methods have a spiritual quality that is foreign to the Hollywood concept of heroism.

During the Golden Age of the German cinema, in the Twenties, Fritz Lang also developed a distinctive epic style. In *The Niebelungen* (released in two parts as *Siegfried*, 1924, and *Kriemhild's Revenge*, 1924), Lang's expressionist *mise en scène* enhanced the heroic *motifs* of the medieval epic of Siegfried's adventures and Kriemhild's vengeance. Lang treated his classic source in a highly stylised manner, with extreme chiaroscuro lighting, exaggerated camera angles, and stately, rigidly symmetrical compositions such as in the representative scene in which soldiers are lined up in neat rows against a blank sky, their arches poised in immaculate patterns. In the battle scenes, the conflicts of plane and direction of movement are as schematic as in Eisenstein. Lang uses architecture for its formal, decorative properties but also to underscore the Germanic themes of destiny and entrapment. His employment of architectural details, in which

Two shots from the classic Odessa Steps sequence, in Eisenstein's Battleship Potemkin, *1925. Eisenstein's montage theory was based on unrelenting visual conflict; the stills here demonstrate sharp contrasts between long shot and close-up, and between horizontal and vertical composition.*

The heroic Siegfried, riding through a heavily stylized, studio-created forest, in Fritz Lang's 1924 film of The Niebelungen.

arches, columns, and the texture of walls and ceilings often function as a powerful evocation of a primitive, violent society, is in many ways an anticipation of Eisenstein's *mise en scène* in *Ivan the Terrible*.

Lang's style is heavily ornamental, richly and self-consciously pictorial: practically every shot could be presented as a still in a photography exhibit. The world the film creates is artificial, studio-bound; objective reality is rigorously excluded, or distorted, as in most of the German films of the period. The concept of character is similarly formal. As in Eisenstein, the characters are types, icons. Our first view of Siegfried is on his horse cantering through a stylised, sun-dappled forest. Enclosed by sun and fog, he seems to have materialised out of the elements. Abstracted from the real world, the *mise en scène* lends an immediate aura of legend, and the blond, handsome Siegfried becomes the visual apotheosis of a legendary hero. The forest setting is sufficiently removed from reality so that Siegfried's fight with the dragon does not seem intrusive. Lang's ethereal atmosphere can

easily contain supernatural elements. American epics, it is significant to note, have by and large avoided the supernatural: Christ walks on the water in Pasolini's *The Gospel According to St. Matthew* (1966), but not in George Stevens's or Nicholas Ray's versions of the life of Christ. In *The Ten Commandments*, supernatural events like the burning bush and the engraving of the commandments by heavenly bolts of fire are conspicuously out of place within the mimetic mode that is standard in Hollywood.

Lang's methods, effective in both a period setting in *The Niebelungen* and in a contemporary one like *Metropolis* (1926), where his handling of crowds is unsurpassed, are too formal for American epics. The constructivist sets and the rigidly orchestrated movement of masses counter American predilections for physical reality and for the autonomy of the individual. As Siegfried Kracauer notes in *From Caligari to Hitler: a Psychological History of the German Film*, the extreme visual formality of the German expressionist films of the Twenties anticipates Leni Riefenstahl's monumental compositions in *The Triumph of the Will* (1934). The Nazi filmmaker reduces the human figure to an abstract element in a grand symmetrical design. Visually, Hitler's robot-like legions recall the oppressed workers in *Metropolis*. The German taste for figures

Fellini's hallucinatory visions of ancient Rome, in Satyricon, *1969.*

arranged for ornamental or political impact is surely symptomatic, as Kracauer suggests, of a national failing that allowed for the rise of Hitler.

The expressionist *mise en scène* of Lang's German epics did, however, trickle into American films—in the Forties *film noir*, though, rather than in the epic. The *genre's* menacing world of criss-crossing shadows, darkened city streets, and ominous staircases, expressed a mood of American postwar anxiety, though the films were often directed by German expatriates like Robert Siodmak and Lang himself. The doom-ridden *films noirs*, in which fate pursues a series of hapless heroes as relentlessly as it does Siegfried, found congenial the German syntax for expressing the macabre.

In Germany in the Twenties, epics dramatised fatalistic themes, whereas the epic form was prominent in American films in the teens and Twenties and again in the Fifties during periods of prosperity. In the Forties, at a time of national disillusionment, American films co-opted the visual style that the Germans had used in the silent period as a means of enhancing epic material; the different uses made of expressionist technique suggest a fundamental gap between German and American sensibilities.

In revisionist, experimental depictions of the ancient world during the sound film era, it is the Italians who once again have led the way with epic material. *Fellini's Satyricon* (1969) and Pasolini's *Medea* (1971), for stunning examples, are imaginative re-creations of ancient societies that challenge the standard Hollywood literalness. Free from studio pressure, Fellini and Pasolini have rendered ancient Rome and Greece as a series of nightmarish distortions of architecure and landscape. The images in both films are hallucinatory and apocalyptic; the films have a savagery, a sense of danger, that would never be permitted in a Hollywood epic. Both directors have pierced the visual conventions, as well as the sense of order, that prevail in the traditional epic, replacing these with entirely new rhythms and sounds, so that ancient Romans in *Satyricon* and ancient Greeks in *Medea* seem genuinely strange and remote—creatures from another planet. The characters move in rapid, erratic patterns, making bizarre sounds that have an incantatory rhythm. Tribal, pre-literate activites are presented as rituals for which we don't have an explanatory code. The wild *décor*—the strange cave-like dwellings, the almost supernatural, other-worldly landscapes—with its continual prom-

ise of violence, gives both films the aura of science fiction. These strange new worlds gradually overtake us.

Both films have the fluid movement of dreams, and both seem like the expression of their directors' private fantasies. Orgiastic, glittering, riotous, *Satyricon* is the most extravagant of Fellini's fantasies of decadence. It is a film almost entirely without human feeling; the director's concern is instead reserved for *mise en scène*, for colour and spectacle, and the result is an epic bash.

Pasolini's *The Gospel According to St. Matthew* counters Hollywood spectacle in the other direction, not by being more anarchic and free-form than an American major studio epic could ever be, but by being more austere. Pasolini removes all the make-up from the characters in Christ's story. The faces are not those of Hollywood, but of simple country people. The extras all look parched and weathered. The buildings are bare, the desert doesn't look like a Promised Land, or a Hallmark Card rendering of the Holy Land, but is instead truly barren, unyielding, forbidding. The visual austerity is echoed in Pasolini's interpretation of Christ as a Marxist revolutionary. This Christ is not a humane teacher but a humourless young radical. Pasolini's *Gospel* has the detachment of Brechtian epic theatre, and like Brecht, Pasolini uses the alienation technique to point up moral and political lessons. To counter the usual pathos aimed for in Hollywood religious epics, Pasolini distances the drama with the anachronistic use of contemporary African music and "modern" film techniques like the zoom and the jump cut. The film has the nervous, jagged rhythm of Godard's *Breathless*. The sermons are presented simply, and directly to the audience, with fades setting off chapter and verse. As Christ speaks against a blank background, changes in lighting denote the passage of time.

Roberto Rossellini has also experimented with severe interpretations of epic materials in films like *The Rise of Louis XIV* (1966) and *Socrates* (1970). Rossellini's view of Renaissance France and of ancient Greece involves an adaptation of neo-realist techniques to historical reconstruction. Both films have a radically different pace from the Hollywood spectacle. Rossellini's deliberate, almost slow-motion rhythm provides a kind of scrim between audience and film; the pacing itself becomes a means of historical distancing. Both films are filled with naturalistic detail. In the opening scene of

Louis XIV, the camera, operating as an objective reporter, follows a servant on her early morning chores; the calmly recorded domestic detail recalls the opening of De Sica's *Umberto D*. Once the royal figures enter, Rossellini's film proceeds in the same casual manner, as if history were a matter of getting up in the morning, putting on clothes, eating, opening doors. The film adheres to none of the narrative conventions of movies about royalty. Rossellini resolutely removes the layers of myth that have accumulated around the French King. Louis XIV is played by an entirely unprepossessing actor who speaks in a quiet monotone; we become eavesdroppers on history, which is presented as a sequence of unheroic actions by unexceptional people.

Socrates, challenging the Hollywood conception of ancient Greece, is planned as a series of close-ups. It is a severe film that thwarts audience involvement. Because its lengthy monologues are filmed in single takes punctuated by a repetitive zooming camera, the film forces the audience to notice its technique, and dramatic values are sacrificed for Rossellini's absorption with a set of limited visual experiments. The director's treatment of a tragic theme is unwaveringly intellectual; and, as in *Louis XIV*, the denial of expectations forces us to see historical characters in fresh perspectives.

Rossellini approaches potentially epic material by avoiding all the visual *clichés* and customary narrative patterns of the epic film. His austere, precise manner and the sobriety and understatement of his actors, impart a neo-realistic texture to his interpretations of historical figures.

Robert Bresson has also countered Hollywood excess in his bare period films like *The Trial of Joan of Arc* (1961) and *Lancelot du Lac* (1974). Bresson's lean, spare recreation of the Middle Ages is a startling contrast to the Metro-Goldwyn-Mayer pastry of pictures like *Ivanhoe* (1952) and *The Knights of the Round Table* (1954). Bresson's Middle Ages is evoked through minimal details of setting and atmosphere, and only Bergman's *Virgin Spring* (1959) and *The Seventh Seal* (1957) compare to it as an expression of a harsh, unyielding medieval sensibility. In his film about Joan, Bresson suggests spiritual transcendence through an absolute minimum of means. In avoiding the expressionist elements that Dreyer depended on in his version of Saint Joan, Bresson has created one of the most austere films ever made. He achieves transcendence

by constricting his frame; his approach seems totally artless, unadorned, yet its unbroken succession of flat images, neutral camera positions, and static compositions, attains power through accumulation. Bresson's method of conveying Joan's ineffable otherworldliness is a kind of reprimand to Hollywood's attempts to achieve religious exaltation through an overabundance of means, with colour, the packed frame, stereophonic sound, symphonic orchestras and enormous choirs performing thunderous scores by Miklos Rosza or Dmitri Tiomkin.

Luchino Visconti is another Italian film-maker whose operatic style, absorption with the past, and passionate interest in *décor*, mark him as a director of epics. His infatuation with sensuous surfaces is certainly more typical of the Italians' delight in epics than Rossellini's austerity, which is something of an aberration in the history of Italian art. Visconti, however, never made the fully realised epic that his combination of interests promised. *The Leopard* (1963) is his most assured statement in the epic mode, yet it was so badly disfigured in its dubbed English version that it is impossible to evaluate fairly. Giuseppe di Lampedusa's novel provided Visconti with the large social theme that he always favoured: an aristocratic way of life in Eighteenth-century Sicily is eroded by powerful new social forces; a prominent family enacts the conflict between generations that threatens collapse to the *ancien régime*. The film's centrepiece is a grand ball in which the private and public dramas merge in a series of encounters between characters of different social classes and political beliefs. Elegantly filmed, with a swooping, encircling camera, the long scene is a textbook of *mise en scène*.

Among Visconti's films with modern subjects, *The Damned* (1969) is most nearly epic in theme and treatment. Through the history of a powerful family, Visconti constructs a fierce indictment of the moral chaos of early Hitlerian Germany. Performed in an operatic style characteristic of Visconti's final, rococo manner, the film is filled with images of decadence.

Visconti's style, like that of other prominent Italian directors of his generation, modulated from neo-realism to fantasy. He shifted his focus from oppressed working people in *La terra trema* (1947) and *Ossessione* (1942) to the rich, jaded characters of his final films. His early neo-realist dramas, with their long takes and deliberate pacing, had a grey, intensely naturalistic texture altogether foreign to the visual explosiveness of his late films like *The Damned* and *Ludwig* (1973). As the scope of his films expanded in the direction of epic, Visconti became more absorbed in surfaces, and social consciousness grew subservient to *décor*. Visconti clearly felt he needed to match his large themes with extravagance of design and performance. He began to put on spectacular shows that released fantasies which had built up over a lifetime. Films like *The Damned* and *Ludwig* look like coded essays in homo-eroticism. As Visconti's visual style escalated to baroque proportions, as he courted the grand manner and allowed his work to become encrusted with a layer of camp and titillation, he was a less serious and controlled artist than he had been at the beginning of his career, as a pioneer neo-realist. For Visconti, the vastness of the epic milieu threatened his integrity as an artist.

Sergio Leone's Italian westerns are closer to American epics in subject matter than the work of other Italian directors like Pasolini or Visconti, but Leone uses American *motifs* only in order to spin delirious variations on them. His *Once Upon a Time in the West* (1969) is a burlesque of westerns realised with such elegance as to become a celebration of the *genre*, as adulatory and as self-consciously mythic as *Shane* (1953). The story is a conglomeration of cliches built on the archetypal revenge theme; but Leone's real interest is in the formal surfaces of the *genre*, which he treats with balletic grace. Every action, every encounter, is treated with climactic significance. Each scene is enlarged by the swirling, craning, endlessly gliding camera; Leone is a serious rival to Ophüls in his infatuation with long takes and continuity achieved through movement within the frame. The complex interaction between the movement of the actors and the movement of the camera amounts to a cinematic choreography in which every gesture is deliberately italicised, and prolonged almost to the point of self-parody. The film's lush atmosphere is aided by the grand cadences of Ennio Morrecone's score.

Once Upon a Time in the West is a series of monumental images based on the iconography of American-made westerns but surpassing them in size and luxuriousness. Made by an American, the film would probably look like a send-up of the *genre* (such as Mel Brooks's *Blazing Saddles)*; but Leone directs with so much passion that the film becomes an exploration of epic style. A conventional revenge drama is transformed into an epic on the taming of the West. The final scenes of the coming of the railroad to an isolated landscape represent the incursions of civilisation on the fierce milieu in which the revenge story has been enacted. Leone's seductive style has expanded the threadbare script, thereby vindicating the power of *mise en scène* to enhance and even to create theme. The film is less a triumph of form over content than a rare instance in which style magnifies a lean idea. It is an exhilarating display of epic temperament.

Japanese epics also seem like variations on American westerns; and it is interesting to note that the greatest Japanese epic, Kurosawa's *Seven Samurai* (1954), was the basis of an American film called *The Magnificent Seven* (1960). Kurosawa's long film has a simple story: a village of farmers is threatened by bandits, and the terrorised community employs seven samurai to defend its land. This basic framework is given epic elaboration as Kurosawa presents an overview of Sixteenth-century Japanese society. The film vividly presents the clash between social classes, revealing the code that governs the conduct of each class. The confrontation between bandits and samurai is elaborated to the point where it serves as a symbolic contest between two philosophies of life.

The film is concerned with details: of the method of selection of the samurai, of the samurai's plans of attack and defence, of the life of the village. The accumulation of detail gives the film its aura of ritual.

Kurosawa treats the past with great respect—he accepts its validity—and with a rigorous realism. He uses the past to embroider a modern philosophical statement. The chief samurai, and the hero of the film, is a wise stoic who inspires worship in the younger men who want to serve him and to fight alongside him. Like the archetypal hero of the American West, he does what he has to do in order to preserve his honour. He is without illusions since he knows that the villagers will forget him once he saves them from the bandits; yet he approaches the defence of the village with great pride in his skills. He is an unusually knowing epic hero who represents for the other samurai an image of absolute stability. Rationalistic and sceptical, he is yet something of an idealist as well.

Kurosawa's long and elaborately detailed film handles its epic trappings with great control and economy. The battle scenes have a harsh beauty; the long, concluding battle in the rain is masterfully (and unobtrusively) edited. Kurosawa punctuates the action with horizontal compositions in the epic mould—long shots of warriors framed against the sky; moving shots of hordes of galloping horses; the village, shrouded in fog and mist, observed in extreme long shot. The film is constantly in movement, either through the tracking, craning camerawork or the stampeding warriors. The picture has an entirely unforced rhythm, its epic effects treated in an understated manner. As a director of epic, Kurosawa is resolutely unexotic; he is perhaps the most unself-conscious of the foreign masters of epic style. His work is remarkably spare, and yet the experience of seeing *Seven Samurai* has the fullness and density that are prerequisites of the epic.

4. Moral and Religious Epics

Filled with action and variety of incident, epics tell stories about superheroes. They are meant to entertain, but also to instruct and ennoble. The two great epics in world literature, Homer and the Bible, contain the inherited wisdom of generations of the ancient Greeks and Hebrews, and they therefore express deep-rooted tribal values; their stories, based on history or at least on a kind of fundamental psychological truth, teach by precept and example, and their heroes behave according to an inherited world view evolved out of generations of experience. The Homeric and Biblical heroes are basically exemplary, and though, like Job or Noah or Achilles or Ulysses, they are flawed, they ultimately act in such a way as to vindicate the ideal as it was conceived by the ancients. In the Renaissance, the Homeric heroes were regarded as embodying supreme virtues of manliness, courage, and endurance, and the Homeric poems were used as manuals for the conduct of the ideal man.

Enshrining characters and events that play a crucial role in the evolution of a religion or a nation, epics are celebratory and affirmative. Created out of a communal consciousness, epics are a public, official art with broad social purposes. Epics are meant to unite the community, to heal and uplift. But at the same time epic authors like Homer and the Old Testament prophets are often sceptics who honour the past in order to excoriate the present. In *The Waste Land*, T. S. Eliot uses an epic technique by contrasting classical themes with shabby contemporary characters and settings in order to underscore the hollowness of the modern age.

Ever backward-looking, epics are written to deify central historical or religious events and to discover through them some moral or political theme that has contemporary application. Epics, then, use the past to celebrate a major event in the evolution of a social, religious, political, or national community. True epics on film, like their oral or literary progenitors, also reconstruct the past in a way that goes beyond the intent simply to be entertaining or spectacular. The genuine epic has a lofty purpose, a reason for being higher than that of accurate historical reconstruction. The full-fledged epic uses the past to illuminate the present, or to reveal timeless themes of religious transcendence and heroic responses to catastrophes like war. Epics employ the past in creative ways in order to offer warnings, reminders, consolations to the audience.

Epics therefore have some kind of didactic underpinning. In films, this moralistic strain was more obviously manifest in the silent period. The lesson-pointing, however, was no clear-cut index of quality, since *Intolerance*, the greatest American epic, is also among the most moralistic, while Ince's *Civili-*

zation, equally passionate in its desire to instruct, is among the most foolish.

A principal strategy of these message-bearing silent epics was to present their stories in parallel segments set in different time periods. The bifurcated construction of films like *Intolerance, Civilization, The Ten Commandments,* and *Noah's Ark* (as well as lesser DeMille films like *Madame Satan,* (1930) is designed to make sure that the audience sees the relevance of the story set in ancient times. The period contrasts between ancient Egypt, say, and modern Manhattan, promote the idea that history repeats itself and that the present age, therefore, can profit from historical examples.

Griffith's spectacular experiment with parallel editing in *Intolerance* set the comparison-contrast pattern. The film presents four separate stories, and the abrupt displacements in time and place express

Griffith's thematic intent in a direct way. The film's four stories, which represent varying examples of man's "intolerance," provide the parallel texts of the director's sermon. The three historical stories—the fall of Babylon; the Crucifixion; the St. Bartholomew's Day Massacre—are concerned with defeat and oppression. The collapse of Babylon is caused by power-mad priests who betray their King to the Persians; Christ is mocked and crucified by the Romans; in medieval France, the Protestants slaughter the Huguenots. Only in the modern story, "The Mother and the Law," are the victimised characters saved.

The narratives are not precisely parallel in theme, since only the Crucifixion and the St. Bartholomew's Day Massacre are clear-cut instances of intolerance. The other two stories are about greed rather than intolerance; the ambitious priests in "The Fall of

Queen Catherine and her court, from "The St. Bartholomew's Day Massacre" episode in Intolerance. *Of the film's four separate but parallel episodes, Griffith was least interested in this one.*

Babylon" resemble the capitalists of big business and of the underworld in the modern story. But the general theme of oppression links the stories; and Griffith introduces a *leitmotif* of a woman rocking a cradle to suggest thematic continuity.

Each story, on its own, is filled with the maudlin sentimentality, the dependence on coincidence, and the naïve overstatement that are the residue of Griffith's training in and sympathy for the conventions of the Nineteenth-century popular theatre. Except for the Christ story, Griffith uses familiar means to heighten audience involvement: he places little people in big settings. His three heroines—Brown Eyes in the medieval French episode, the Mountain Girl in the Babylon sequence, and the Dear One in the modern story—are pushed to the forefront of the action in order to give popular audiences characters to identify with. The virginal, high-spirited, victimised child-women are designed to represent the fate of average people in extraordinary circumstances. Prosaic and homespun as they are, however, Griffith's leading ladies do not reduce the scope of the film because they are silent and because they are never allowed space enough to compete with Griffith's monumental blueprint. The "idea" is the film's true hero, in a more explicit way perhaps than in any other major American film—Griffith places his stereotyped figures as icons in his vast tapestry.

Considered individually, the stories are commonplace, and the director is really interested in only two of them, "The Fall of Babylon" and "The Mother and the Law". The other two fragments are included for thematic reinforcement, filling out the design by multiplying historical events that support the theme. The Christ scenes, a series of beautifully lit *tableaux*, are particularly remote. Framed by halo lighting and photographed in blurred focus, Christ is a majestic figure who barely participates in worldly events. Griffith's distant and reverential treatment established a pattern for the presentation of Christ on film; like several later versions of the Christ story, *Intolerance* maintains an attitude of unquestioning awe. Griffith selects central events from Christ's life—the wedding at Cana, the encounter with Mary Magdalene, the miracle of turning water into wine, Calvary, and the Crucifixion—to serve as footnotes to the two main stories.

The St. Bartholomew Massacre is not as carefully composed as the brief scenes from the Greatest Story. Griffith is barely interested in this episode on any level, and he settles for broad caricature in his depiction of an almost comically evil Queen Catherine and of his dewy heroine Brown Eyes and her noble *fiancé*. This segment of the film has energy only in its scenes of the massacre where the imagery of slaughter parallels the Persian army's attack on Babylon.

There is far more human and visual interest in the two principal narratives. Enhanced by Mae Marsh's impassioned performance as the Dear One, the modern story is the most gripping of the four. Mae Marsh's character, who changes in the course of the story from a giddy young girl to a mature, devoted wife, effectively embodies Griffith's theme that love will ultimately triumph over intolerance. Her acting has an intensity that infuses melodrama with lyric and tragic overtones.

The epic quality of "The Fall of Babylon," on the other hand, is more visual than emotional. The immense outdoor set of the palace forecourt is built on a scale that is destined, because of economics, to remain unsurpassed. Rising a hundred feet above a rural Hollywood, the walls and towers are festive as well as grand. An elephant *motif* introduces a playful quality to the monumental structure; poised for show on their hind legs, the elephants seem like Griffith's own personal embellishment of ancient architectural design. Griffith and his cameraman, Billy Bitzer, worked for days to set up a crane shot in which the camera moves from a high angle long shot of the Babylonian victory celebration to a close-up of doves pulling a chariot; the graceful downward movement of the camera is stunning, the most virtuoso touch in this most virtuoso of films. Griffith displays his elaborate set sparingly, and there are times when we could wish that he would temporarily forget his solemn purpose in order to linger on details of the set and on the hive of human activity that swells within it. The Babylon set connotes a magnificent bygone Hollywood; it's an emblem of the Hollywood epic at its earliest, and highest, point of elaboration.

In an effort to recoup his losses on the film, Griffith released "The Fall of Babylon" and "The Mother and the Law" separately; but neither film is as effective on its own as it is when seen as part of Griffith's great mosaic concept. For the true epic scope that the film has is derived almost entirely from its audacious parallel structure. Cross-cutting gives the film's idea its epic thrust and enforces Griffith's didactic theme. The spectacular moments

D.W. GRIFFITH'S
DRAMATIC THUNDERBOLT
"THE MOTHER AND THE LAW"

THE LITTLE DEAR ONE.

Mae Marsh as The Little Dear One, from "The Mother and the Law" episode in Intolerance. *Mae Marsh's immense perform-ance lends epic stature to melodramatic material.*

are enlarged by Griffith's method of visual linkage. The paralleling technique yields a stunning climax in which the last-minute rescue of the modern story is contrasted with the Persian armies thundering toward Babylon, with the massacre of the Huguenots, and with the Crucifixion. To heighten tension, Griffith emphasises visual conflicts be-tween shots. (The collision effect he achieved was to have a profound impact on Eisenstein's theory of montage.) Griffith changes the direction of move-ment from shot to shot, so that if the Persian army swirls across the screen from left to right, the governor's train in the following shot will be photo-graphed speeding across the frame from right to left. Griffith varies the lengths of the shots; shots be-come shorter as he approaches his parallel cli-maxes, and the movement within shots grows more

hectic as well. The charge of the army, the lone car racing to catch the train in the modern story, the massacre of the innocents, and the Crucifixion are blended by Griffith's dynamic cross-cutting into one of the great finales in film history, a sequence of surging visual rhythm.

Griffith underlines his allegorical intent by con-cluding the film with scenes meant to portray universal peace and brotherhood: prisons dissolve into open fields, a battleground is transformed into a picnic area where two angelic children embrace while a heavenly host of angels confers its blessing. The imagery is florid and inorganic; the pacifist theme seems forced. But Griffith intended his spec-tacle to be a sermon against war and oppression (and, on a more personal level, as a refutation of those who accused him of being himself intolerant because of the treatment of blacks in *The Birth of a Nation*); and, for him, the grandiose imagery at the end was a way of underlining his moral purpose. But even with this help at the finale, audiences at the time were confused by the film's elaborate structure; they failed to get the point.

Many films have been influenced by *Intolerance*, but none has tried to imitate its intensely cinematic form. *2001: A Space Odyssey* probably has the closest formal similarities to Griffith's monumental concept. *Intolerance* was the first great Hollywood epic, and *2001* is, to date, the last. The two films define the grand possibilities of epic form in film; both have enormous scope and both use, to spectacular effect, the resources of film for juggling time and space and for linking parallel actions in widely separated settings. The two films, in essence, take the world for their setting, and the entire history of man for their time span. They are Hollywood's two great cosmic epics in which time and place become, in a direct way, the film-makers' true subjects. Yet neither film, though each has had numerous local influence, spawned imitations because they were too grand and, curiously enough, too personal and idiosyncratic, to inaugurate a sub-*genre* of movie epics.

Intolerance and *2001* are the kind of pure cinema that the epic format would seem to (but seldom does) promote. In both films, the themes are expressed directly through such formal concerns as editing, narrative construction, and the manipulation of time and place. Both films startled and puzzled their original audiences; and though in each case the paraphrasable content of what each director wanted to say is simple enough, his meaning was inseparable from the films' complex, revolutionary structure and their radical use of the possibilities of film punctuation.

Like Griffith, Kubrick wants to suggest connections between historical cycles. In order to link the dawn of man with a futuristic space age, he uses a breathtaking match cut between a prehistoric bone-become-weapon and a spaceship gracefully circling the earth. Kubrick's cut, which associates objects almost infinitely separated in space and time, is like a rediscovery of the power of editing that Griffith was working on so majestically in *Intolerance*. Like *Intolerance*, *2001* spans man's history in order to point a moral lesson. Both films are journeys through time that seek to demonstrate man's essential sameness and the inevitably cyclic nature of history. Both films promote elementary philosophical precepts: *Intolerance* dramatises man's recurrent inhumanity to man, *2001* ironically pits prehistoric

and modern man's imperfect conquest of his environment against an omnipresent extra-terrestrial intelligence. In both movies, the individual is controlled by cosmic and intransigent forces such as history, destiny, and technology. In *2001*, the vastness of outer space resembles Griffith's mammoth Babylon in reducing the individual to a mere speck.

Like Griffith's epic, *2001* has a fragmented structure, though the film's episodes are presented linearly rather than simultaneously. The dawn of man, the briefing at the space station, the moon landing, the trip to Jupiter and Beyond are connected elliptically; on a first viewing, the links between the episodes seem especially vague, with only a tangential narrative logic to bind them. Like Griffith, however, Kubrick depends on a visual *leitmotif* to provide thematic continuity: the ominous black obelisk that appears in the climax of the main episodes is a kind of visual equivalent to the cradle endlessly rocking that links the separate strands of *Intolerance*.

The obelisk, filmed from an extreme low angle to emphasise its power, links the apes to the lone astronaut sequestered in the glacial *Louis quinze* bedroom. Both films thus return to the same images to underline thematic connections. The closing shot in *2001*, of the starchild afloat in space, echoes the film's opening shot of the earth outlined against the moon.

Griffith wanted his thesis in *Intolerance* to be absolutely clear, and he was amazed when the mass audience for which he had made the film was puzzled by it. His elastic use of film had transformed his content; his simple, even naïve concept, was presented in a radical style for which filmgoers were unprepared. Kubrick's manner and intent are more evenly matched. His long takes and gracefully circling camera are used like Griffith's rapid cross-cutting to suggest the repetitions and cyclical patterns that mark human "progress." The film's stately pace yields meanings reluctantly, piecemeal, but the main outline of Kubrick's argument is clear. The director's vision of the future (as well as the remote past) is richly ironic and disapproving; his presentation of man's development from ape to technocrat is sharply satirical. Through his misuse of technology, man has become depersonalised; the computer HAL is more lively and has more temperament than the bland astronauts. But man's relation to the extra-terrestrial force represented by the threatening

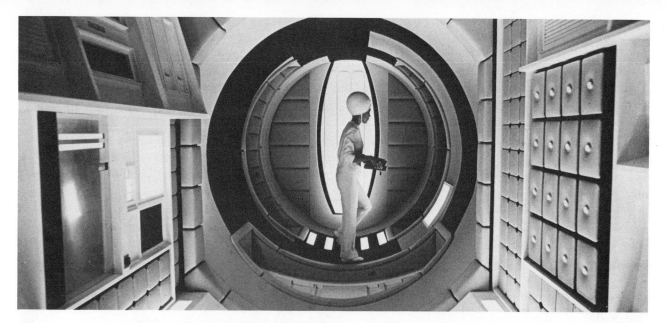

*Images of man's imprisonment in an impersonal futuristic space
age, in Stanley Kubrick's awesome* 2001: A Space Odyssey,
1968.

obelisk remains enigmatic. The film's last great section, in which the astronaut's trip to the Infinite is conveyed through aerial views of psychedelically coloured landscapes that recall the vastness and isolation of the film's first segment, has a suggestive power that works almost subliminally. Unlike *Intolerance*, Kubrick's final message is cryptic, unutterable. To decipher the significance of the film's closing images—the appearance of the obelisk in the elegant, spare bedroom, the final metamorphosis of the astronaut from extreme old age to foetus—is almost to defile them, for Kubrick has created a deliberately open-ended epic to which no final, decoded meaning can be assigned. And it is that sense of the infinite, in time and space as well as in theme, that gives the film its monumental quality and that makes it an epic unlike any other.

Intolerance and *2001* share the didactic intent of the traditional epic storyteller. They are both moralistic epics that transcend the boundaries of a single place and time. They are the most ambitious epics in American films for which their directors, respectively, expanded and re-discovered the possibilities of, film editing.

★

Griffith and Kubrick make masterful use of historical contrast, but usually the contrast technique has been heavy-handed. With considerably less success than in *Intolerance* and *2001*, DeMille's *Ten Commandments*, Michael Curtiz's *Noah's Ark*, and Ince's *Civilization* all employ a bifurcated structure in order to enforce a moral lesson. In *The Ten Commandments* (1923 version), the history of Moses serves as prologue to a modern story which dramatises the contemporary relevance of the commandments. Two brothers are compared; one observes the commandments, and prospers, the other is a rebel, and his career traces the pattern of rise and fall that was to become standard in the gangster cycle in the Thirties.

In *Civilization*, a modern story that is a parable about a totalitarian society which wages war, is bisected by the story of Christ. Christ enters the contemporary drama, and His elevated example as the Prince of Peace changes the course of the world by diverting mankind from its pursuit of war and conquest.

In *Noah's Ark*, the Biblical tale of the flood is interrupted by a flashforward set in Europe during the First World War. To connect the ancient cataclysm to the modern one, the characters in the war drama are played by the same actors as in the Biblical parable.

These three films, typical of the silent period in their sentimentality and extravagance, are naïve yet powerful sermons. All three vividly depict a world plunged into chaos: the orgy and the earthquake in *The Ten Commandments*, the scenes of war in *Civilization* and in the modern section of *Noah's Ark*, the flood in the ancient story. The films each dramatise the wrath of God against His erring people, and apocalyptic scenes of upheaveal and destruction contain a ferocious moralistic zeal. The big scenes are designed as warnings, and yet they have a direct appeal to the senses that competes with but never entirely obscures the moralistic intent. Audiences, clearly, are supposed to be "better off" after seeing the films; they are supposed to be checked in their tendencies to wickedness and to disobedience of the commandments. The thrust of these visual sermons, therefore, is deeply conservative, and pragmatic: film is being used as moral propaganda, just as dictators like Lenin and Hitler recognised the possibilities of epic cinema for political propaganda.

The silent epics, of course, mix morality with commerce since the films were after all made to earn money. DeMille's film in particular was catered to the marketplace; the high-minded prologue, in fact, was decided upon as an afterthought, as a shrewd means of boosting the commonplace modern story. But these three representative films do have a sense of purpose rare in sound epics. In tone and theme, as well as in narrative structure, the films reflect the taste of a particular era. Except for a rare exception like *2001* (a special case in many ways), the bifurcated method is a silent film technique. When De Mille's *Sign of the Cross* was re-released in 1939, it was preceded by a modern prologue in which an airplane with a carefully chosen crew of Allied forces flies over modern Rome, thereby pointing a parallel between Hitler and Nero as two mad tyrants. DeMille's original film opens with the burning of Rome as Nero strums his lyre and cackles insanely. The prologue links the ancient conflagration to the modern one; the ancient besieged city becomes a mirror of the modern Occupation. The prologue seemed strained to most critics in 1939—this kind of lesson-pointing was a more organic part of the syntax of the silent screen.

62

Cause and effect: preparing for war, and a devastated war-torn landscape, in Ince's stern moral fable, Civilization, *1916.*

★

Without using the contrast method, many epic films have drawn on the moralistic base of the didactic silent epics. Like *The Ten Commandments* and *Noah's Ark*, epics often dramatise key moments in the development of Judaism and Christianity because religious subjects have an immediate significance and also certify the seriousness of a film's intent. Hollywood always knew that the religious big time could sell tickets.

Christ Himself has been the centre of interest of only a few films, but Christianity has supplied the background for many films that aspire to epic stature. Griffith was only marginally concerned with the story of Christ in *Intolerance*, but his treatment of Christ had a great influence on the way Hollywood films have approached sacred text. Griffith presents Christ as a mystical figure, more legend and symbol than flesh-and-blood man. Griffith's Christ is a

H. B. Warner's magisterial Christ, in DeMille's surprisingly restrained King of Kings, *1927.*

remote figure dispensing wisdom and justice with statesque gestures. He is more an aspect of the director's radiant *mise en scène* than a dramatic character.

DeMille's *King of Kings* continues the painterly quality of Griffith's early treatment of a divine subject. The film begins shakily, in Mary Magdalene's gaudy house, the perfect *kitsch* setting for a DeMille orgy. But the eager vulgarity of the opening is misleading, for the film is the most reverent and the most stylistically consistent of the director's large-scale projects. Once Christ enters—in a beautiful scene, we "see" Him first through the wonder registered on the face of a young girl—the film behaves itself entirely. Critics have often questioned DeMille's sincerity, but the director's claims of devoutness are apprent in this film. *King of Kings* is a stately religious pageant made to celebrate Jesus

A blind girl approaches the Messiah, in King of Kings. *To convey a religious aura, DeMille uses exquisite* chiaroscuro *lighting throughout the film.*

64

and to inspire belief in His works. More internal and circumspect than any of DeMille's other films, *King of Kings* is one of the genuinely religious Hollywood epics.

As always in American films concerning Christ, the picture is deeply conservative since it wants to confirm rather than to disturb the preconceptions of a mass audience. There is nothing idiosyncratic in DeMille's reading of the Gospels. His Christ, like Griffith's, is a kindly, paternal figure serenely aloof from politics and society. The principal events from the Gospel are dramatised, as if on cue; the film is a kind of Sunday school re-enactment of high points from the New Testament given the finest Hollywood production values.

There are only a few eccentric touches (Pilate's huge throne is in the form of an eagle with its wings outspread) and only a few extravagant details in costume and *décor* that recall the usual DeMille milieu; but for the most part this is a solemn, straightforward presentation. The silence, as for so many other epic subjects, is to the film's advantage. DeMille's mute Christ gestures grandly, though not with the exaggerated flourishes typical of much silent screen acting, and the silence, together with the cathedral-like lighting, gives the iconography a timeless quality. The silence provides a necessary distance from the divine hero, and frees the director from discovering fresh or interesting interpretations for Christ's sermons.

The two major sound treatments of Christ, Nicholas Ray's *King of Kings* and George Stevens's *The Greatest Story Ever Told*, struggle with the problems of language. Both films confront the challenge of presenting Christ's teachings in a way that compels us to react to the speeches as original thoughts rather than familiar quotations. Both films also work harder than DeMille's to find a visual idiom in which to present the principal events in Christ's life. Ray and Stevens thus are more concerned than DeMille was to be original and interesting, and perhaps the later film-makers were acknowledging by their creative collaboration with the New Testament that they were making their films in a more sceptical period, at a time when religious values were less central a part of American life. In the late Twenties, DeMille could rely on his audience sharing certain general assumptions about Christianity in a way that, three decades later, Ray and Stevens could not. DeMille did not have to concern himself with whether or not his film would be considered old-fashioned, with whether or not his choice of subject would seem hopelessly reactionary.

Ray's film creates a fuller political context than any of the others. Some of the background is fictional; the attempt is to present Christ as an isolated figure who provokes a seething political holocaust between Rome and Jerusalem. As it fancifully rearranges history, the film invents a few battles, and Christ is often pushed aside to make room for scenes of court intrigue. This is the most worldly of the lives of Christ on film. Jeffrey Hunter was heavily criticised for his performance as the Messiah; he has a light voice, and with his blue eyes and chiselled features he seems almost like a parody of movie star handsomeness, but he plays Christ with a fetching gentleness. A winning, likable Christ may be a superficial conception, though surely not an altogether erroneous one.

Nicholas Ray is a strong, temperamental director, and even with a confused script and much interference from Samuel Bronston, the worried producer, he manages impressive moments: the Sermon on the Mount filmed in a long take, the camera mounted on a descending track; striking high angle shots of the crowds gathered to listen to the Messiah; the Last Supper presented with a fresh visual perspective; the long shadow of Christ at Emmaus at the end; Siobhan McKenna's radiant Virgin Mary. To compete with *Ben-Hur*, Samuel Bronston ordered Ray to embellish the film with spectacle, and the movie ends up providing a case study of how epic themes can be corrupted by inflated budgets.

The Greatest Story Ever Told, on the other hand, represents the summit of the Hollywood epic style. Drawing on his experience in handling panoramic American subjects in *Shane* and *Giant*, Stevens has fashioned a supple visual style that enhances the monumental theme. The recurrent aerial shots that range over vast desert landscapes have real grandeur. Stevens uses fluid dissolves in cross-cutting from one setting to another or to indicate an indeterminate passage of time; the film has a complex structure, and the frequent parallel editing establishes links between Christ's life and the larger political and social context. As in *Shane*, the director handles landscape lyrically. The deserts, lakes, valleys, and mountains, alternately harsh and lush, provide luminous backdrops. Though he favours silhouettes against dramatic sunsets (which prompted some reviewers to complain that he had

*Two versions of Christ: Jeffrey Hunter as a supremely handso[me]
gentle Saviour in Nicholas Ray's* King of Kings, 1961; *Max [von]
Sydow as the austere, introspective Messiah in George Steve[ns']*
The Greatest Story Ever Told, 1965.

Christ (Max von Sydow) being tried by the Sanhedrin, in The Greatest Story Ever Told. *This still is typical of the film's spare and elegant composition.*

rendered Christ's life as a series of picture postcards) and though some scenes duplicate the iconography of familiar paintings, the film has many surprising ideas. The confrontation between Christ and the tempter on a solitary mountaintop is stark and ominous; Salome moves in and out of circles of light as she dances for a solitary, inebriated Herod. Sequences like these have a brooding tension. The raising of Lazarus is photographed from an extreme long shot while on the soundtrack there is a low, insistent buzz, as of a congregation in fervent prayer. After Lazarus's resurrection, the film explodes in a series of rapid cuts as the awed on-lookers joyously proclaim the new Messiah. The settings conscientiously bypass the customary Hollywood opulence, the grey stone of Herod's palace

and courtyard, and of the walls of the city, being appropriately sombre.

Stevens's Christ (Max von Sydow) is notably austere. The actor's lightly accented English sets him apart from the other characters, and his stern face suggests here, as it always does in his work for Ingmar Bergman, layers of spiritual conflict. Like the other American depictions of Christ, the interpretation is fundamentally conservative and external, since Christ remains a largely emblematic figure observed from a distance. But von Sydow's presence deepens the conventional iconography; his performance has intimations of torment and ambiguity. The actor delivers Christ's familiar sermons simply, without any rhetorical flourish, as though he were speaking Christian doctrine for the first time.

Through its spare, striking visual *motifs* and Max von Sydow's integrity, the film transcends the limits of its received notions of the meaning of Christ and

Howard Keel, in The Big Fisherman, *1959, one of the many "secondary" religious epics of the 1950s.*

its gimmick of placing famous actors in cameo roles. Stevens's attempt to coat the drama with a religious aura is one of the most successful in American films. There is genuine beauty here, and serenity.

Many Hollywood films with religious themes avoid the problem, which always courts the charge of heresy, of a direct presentation of Christ. This secondary type of religious epic (films like *Ben-Hur, Barabbas, The Silver Chalice, Salome,* and *The Big Fisherman*) swells its own importance by connecting the fate of its characters to that of Christ. The traditional pagan hero of these films that borrow events of the Christian drama normally undergoes a gradual conversion. The paradigmatic heroes of *Quo Vadis?, The Sign of the Cross,* and *The Robe* are Roman officers initially hostile to the new religion. Usually through a romance with a pure but ardent Christian girl, they are chastened, ennobled, and prepared, ultimately, to be martyred in the arena with other believers.

The split between pagan and Christian is a principal theme in Hollywood religious dramas. Often, though, the sincerity of the films has been questioned because the pagans are more vividly depicted than the Christians. As characters in a dramatic story, the sinners are often more convincing then the exemplary characters. Nero and Caligula, played by colourful character actors, frequently steal the show; Charles Laughton's sly, wicked, boyish Nero in *The Sign of the Cross* is much more memorable than the noble Christians played by Elissa Landi and Fredric March. Laughton's few scenes have a biting humour and tension that are missing from the "straight" drama. Peter Ustinov's Nero in *Quo Vadis?* and Jay Robinson's Caligula in *The Robe* and *Demetrius and the Gladiators* sabotage the films, their campy, strutting, vaudevillian performances all but dismantling the inspirational themes. Audiences naturally want to see more of them and less of the pristine heroines and the tormented heroes struggling toward transcendence. American films, for the most part, never learned how

The theatricality of pagan debauchery: Peter Ustinov as the mad Nero, in Quo Vadis?; *Jay Robinson as the equally mad, and equally memorable, Caligula, in* Demetrius and the Gladiators.

to present believers and converts as absorbing characters. Impossibly noble, forbiddingly self-righteous, they are typically presented without nuance or shading. Except in rare instances—Max von Sydow's Christ is one—saints have not been enacted with conviction in American religious epics.

The integrity of the films with Christian themes has been further undermined by Hollywood's inevitable penchant for spectacle. *The Greatest Story Ever Told*, again, is an exception, for though it is a large-scale production, it has none of the lascivious delight in banquets and violence that disfigures reserved-seat religious epics. The big public scenes, however, are usually more engaging than the private drama of the hero's religious progress. Banquets and battles provide the sensuous surfaces that films are inherently attracted to, while religious

transcendence implies stasis, and is thus more easily expressed in a painting—films are concerned with the moment rather than with eternity. Directors like Dreyer, Bresson, and Ozu, who convey a true religious feeling on film, work in a severely contained style. Transcendence, in their work, is achieved cumulatively, through a succession of still moments. Their rigorous, circumscribed style is decidedly unpopular art, and big-budget Hollywood films on religious subjects cannot risk more than a few moments of the kind of visual austerity that signals transcendence in Bresson or Ozu. The severely restrained style is foreign to the Hollywood temper, and most directors of epics like Griffith and DeMille depend for their effects on overabundant means, on visual excess rather than the minimalist cinema of Bresson. The final scene in DeMille's *The Sign of the Cross*, for instance, as the

Rita Hayworth as Salome, *one of many pagan characters transformed by Christianity in New Testament epics of the 1950s.*

characters march up the stairs to the arena, light streaming from above in the form of a cross, is a relatively modest moment; but the preceding activity in the arena, the camera panning midgets, clowns, performing bears, and gladiators, is where the director really lives. The most energetic scene in *The Ten Commandments* is the bacchanal that swirls around the Golden Calf. The orgiastic rites seem to release DeMille from the stiffness of the rest of the film, and the sequence is wonderfully free, light-fingered and exuberant.

Worldliness, sensuality, and decadence, then, are presented with enormous appeal and vigour in many nominally Christian epics. The world of pleasure and of material surfaces is more congenial to the nature of film (and especially to the temper of Hollywood filmmaking) than the inner world of the spirit. The exhibitionism and the display of excess in the scenes of pagan misbehaviour are often the most authentic qualities in the religious films.

Seduced by excess, the films often subvert their inspirational message, but they don't entirely forget it, since even the most godless epic contains scenes that are clearly intended to ennoble. The split between the high and low plots is uneven, however, and the transitions from profane to sacred are often rough. Typical if extreme is the conclusion of *Salome*; in the penultimate scene, Rita Hayworth does a thinly disguised Biblical version of the bump and grind, and in the final scene, primly attired, she listens to the Sermon on the Mount. Terrified of austerity, the American religious film is almost manically expansive; less is decidedly not more, and too much is often not enough. Because the big studios have always been afraid that God and Christ are not enough to sell tickets, elephantiasis afflicts all the religious epics.

And yet there are moments of power and beauty in most of the New Testament spectacles. *Barabbas* is a prime example. The film inflates Pär Lagerkvist's

Anthony Quinn as Barabbas triumphs in the arena over a wicked pagan (Jack Palance). The 1961 film externalises the hero's gradual conversion to Christianity.

simply written novella, giving full treatment to events and settings only sketchily referred to in the original. The climax is set in a colosseum, and the camera, in the DeMille tradition, proudly pans the acrobats, the lions, the gladiators, the swarming crowds; the publicity proclaimed the scene the most spectacular and costly in the history of movies. And yet the events that take place in the colosseum are only incidental to the main theme, an interior one, of the hero's spiritual awakening: over a period of many years, Barabbas the sceptic becomes a true man of God. Lagerkvist's tale is written in a plain style, and since the novelist presents the drama from the hero's own limited point of view, there is a minimum of philosophical and psychological speculation. The film rejects Lagerkvist's austere approach and externalises the theme; still, in Christopher Fry's screenplay, and in Anthony Quinn's performance, there are vestiges of the novella's starkness—images simply and cleanly composed, spare dialogue delivered in a direct manner. The Crucifixion, filmed during an actual eclipse, has an unusual quality, the brooding half-light bathing the images in a mystical aura.

Unlike many of the films with early Christian settings, *Barabbas* is based on distinguished literature. The standard Christian epic is derived from middle-brow best sellers like Lloyd C. Douglas's *The Robe* and *The Big Fisherman*. Douglas's impersonal style more nearly approximates the filmmakers' needs than Lagerkvist's suggestive parable. Film epics, in fact, are seldom based on authetic epic sources. There has been no serious attempt to film *The Iliad* and *The Odyssey*, for instance; Robert Wise's *Helen of Troy* (1956) and an Italian version of *The Odyssey* called *Ulysses* (1953) are like comic strip glosses on Homer. There are successful moments of spectacle in both films: the Cyclops is convincing and frightening; the Trojan Horse is a handsome prop. But the thick texture and mythic resonances of Homeric poetry are missing, and the great stories become, on screen, a series of triumphs for the special effects department.

For Hollywood films, Lloyd C. Douglas and Edna Ferber are more usable than Homer or the Bible. *Cimarron, The Robe, Gone with the Wind, The Silver Chalice,* and *The Egyptian,* for example, provide scope without depth and cover a wide range of subject matter with no literary distinction, so there is no problem of translation, of finding visual equivalents for dense, formulaic language. These "epic" novels are written on the surface, in a prose style immediately accessible to concrete visualisation; and the down-to-earth, stubbornly realistic sensibility of these best-selling potboilers avoids the problem, presented by Homer and the Bible, of how to adapt miraculous and supernatural elements to film. How could the Cyclops, on film, retain the power and mystery it holds over our imaginations through Homer's poetry? How could the gods in Homer, and the God of the Bible, be presented convincingly in a realistic visual medium? Pre-sold properties like *The Robe* and *The Silver Chalice* circumvent these problems by reducing the scale of the religious themes to domestic melodrama handled in a straightforward realistic manner.

In his famous review of *The Robe*, Edmund Wilson wrote that the real purpose of the book—and the reason for its enormous and enduring popularity —was to treat antiquity as though it were contemporary America. Rome and Jerusalem in the time of Christ are presented as typical mid-Western cities; Douglas denies the grandeur, the exoticism and mystery of the ancient world and proceeds imperturbably on the notion that the ancient Romans, after all, were exactly like us. The finicky Roman family in *The Robe* is incorrigibly middle American. Douglas places this family against epochal events—the death of Christ and the spread of Christianity—and the subtext implies that average people too can be touched by, and participate in, history. Douglas (and his millions of readers) are undisturbed by the wild discrepancy between the scale of the book's background events and its puny foreground drama.

Douglas's novel is shrewdly geared to make religion palatable to a broad audience and to tell a story in a way that will interest millions of readers, and as such *The Robe* is conceived on a level ideally suited to a mass-market Hollywood epic. Douglas's provincial inability to see the ancient world as in any way different from contemporary America exactly matches Hollywood's own predisposition.

The film, more fully than the novel, creates a sense of another time, yet the vision remains double: the past is viewed in terms of the present; characters in fancy dress enact a modern pageant about the power of love and religion. Here, as in many of the religious films, sex and love of Christ are closely linked. The reluctant hero is drawn to Christ through his love for a beautiful and seemingly virginal woman. Earthly passion lures him to love of the divine. *The Robe,* as novel and film, is relentlessly tame. It's a safe, craftsmanlike epic potboiler; but it is not the final measure of what Hollywood can do with a big religious subject.

If the problem with films based on New Testament themes is how to portray Christ, the major obstacle in filming Old Testament stories is what to do with God. In the books of the Old Testament, God takes an active role; He is *raisonneur,* guide, master of ceremonies, and as a dramatic character, He is even less viable than Jesus.

In *The Ten Commandments,* the most renowned of the films drawn from the Old Testament, DeMille confronts the challenge of dramatising God and His miraculous works by being as literal as possible. The Red Sea divides; Moses transforms a rod into a snake and turns the sea into blood; the burning bush burns; the commandments are graven into a stone tablet by heavenly bolts of lightning; and God, recorded stereophonically in an echo chamber, speaks to Moses in sepulchral tones. Presenting Biblical miracles as a procession of roadshow special effects, the film becomes a self-infatuated display of Hollywood's technical ingenuity. Working to please a large general audience, however, DeMille probably had no choice but to be exclusively dedicated to the "real." A delicate symbolic method, or restraint in the depiction of miraculous events, would have been risky, since the director had to consider his public as well as his reputation as a master showman.

DeMille's traditional style, though, works against an organic treatment of miracles. Unlike Fellini in *Satyricon,* DeMille hasn't created an exotic environment in which fantastic events can freely take place; DeMille's sober, plodding, conservative manner would seem to rule out the supernatural, but in his own way DeMille is as controlling and manipulative as Fellini; he is a good storyteller who has the ability to make us believe in what he is doing moment by moment, and he manages to introduce miraculous events into the realistic fabric of his film without shattering audience involvement. At its own simple, popular level, the film has power and it makes Biblical legend real and immediate for general audiences.

Celebrating freedom and demonstrating the binding power of the commandments, the film instructs as it entertains. In his own crude manner, DeMille was one of Hollywood's most dedicated moralists. He portrays the delights of sin, but he is always careful to demonstrate the triumph of virtue. Vice in De-

Mille movies has only temporary rewards, while dull virtue endures. The film's neat division between good and evil accords with the Biblical pattern. Moses and Pharaoh are clear-cut embodiments of virtue and vice, integrity and bad faith. As in the Bible, the characters are presented on the surface, with no moral ambiguity. DeMille, a näive moralist, presenting stark conflicts between good and evil, is attracted to the Bible as realistic "living" drama rather than as a series of symbols and legends, and his absolute conviction in his message sustains the film.

The Old Testament, of course, has a more varied texture than the New Testament, since it contains not one hero, but many; not one crucial sequence of events, but many, which cover a vast sweep of time. Yet film-makers have found the New Testament more appealing than the Old Testament legends. Stories based on the life of Christ can be told in the same way over and over; and the Christian theme is so powerful that it elevates almost any fiction, no matter how shopworn, that is placed in front of it. The Old Testament stories require different approaches. The scale of the stories differs too, so that there is not always the opportunity for spectacle that can be relied upon in dramatising the life of Christ.

For the most part, the Old Testament has been plundered by film-makers to provide scenarios of intense romantic conflict. Sex is certainly a more palpable force in the Old Testament than in the New, and Hollywood has ransacked the Hebrew legends for stories like those involving Solomon and Sheba, David and Bathsheba, Samson and Delilah, Esther and the King, the Prodigal Son and the priestess, Ruth and Boaz. Except for the story of Ruth, the films are framed around the figure of the temptress, the Biblical equivalent of the notorious woman in Victorian fiction and the vamp in the Twenties; and the roles have been fashioned as showcases for reigning movie stars, as a chance for their fans to see Hedy Lamarr or Susan Hayward in Biblical fancy dress.

The films do not lose sight of the persistent sin-and-redemption theme, but they have been made to sell romance rather than to point a moral lesson. In these stories, however, romantic involvement has severe consequences. As a result of infatuations, the prodigal son is threatened with the loss of his inheritance; Samson almost loses his strength; David and Solomon are faced with the collapse of their kingdoms. But at the last minute

Two Old Testament couples whose romances have severe consequences: Gregory Peck and Susan Hayward as David and Bathsheba; Yul Brynner and Gina Lollobrigida as Solomon and Sheba.

they are properly guilty about their entanglements and they reclaim their original place in society.

These stories were chosen because of their spectacular trappings as well as for the popular appeal of their star-crossed lovers. The motives are certainly base enough, but the producers had to contend with Biblical themes of temptation and renewal and the films therfore embellish their secular delights with stern moral lessons about civic duty, obedience to God and to His commandments, and Old Testament notions of righteousness.

Unlike the unimaginative and basically contemporary style of these Old Testament romances, John Huston's interpretation of *The Bible . . . in the Beginning* attempts to create visual parallels for Biblical language. Like Biblical diction, the film has a simple, heightened style clearly removed from a mundane or contemporary reality. Beginning with the Creation and concluding with the story of Abraham and Isaac, the film cannot depend like the *Solomon and Sheba* archetype on a nar-

rative with mass popular appeal or on conventional continuity. Huston and his screenwriter, Christopher Fry, stay close to the spirit of Genesis: the dialogue is unadorned yet allusive, and the film doesn't underscore symbolic readings of the symbolically charged material; it dramatises events of cosmic significance in an uncluttered, unselfconscious manner. The film's style, like that of Genesis, is one of grandeur without weightiness. The mystery of Creation, man's fall from innocence, the primal murder, the babble of languages, the flood, God's test of Abraham, are presented with elegant simplicity and a charming, almost childlike, understatement and wonder. Retaining the spareness and economy of the Bible, the film thus attempts to duplicate the abbreviated, "underilluminated" mode that Erich Auerbach describes in *Mimesis* and which he contrasts to the "overilluminated" method of Homer.

The Creation is depicted in a rainbow of pastels. This section, though unsatisfactory, does contain a

Elemental rage: Richard Harris as Cain, in The Bible.

Epic composition: the procession of the animals, two-by-two, from The Noah's Ark *episode, in* The Bible.

kind of awe at the miracle of first beginnings. In the Garden of Eden sequence, the serpent, the tree, and the apple are given a physical materiality that limits their symbolic resonances. The story of Adam's temptation and fall is presented crisply (as in the Bible) without pause for the theological and psychological implications of the relationship between Eve and the serpent and between Adam and Eve. Yet the atmosphere for this section is too realistic (the challenge for the film-maker is to find a style that blends realism with fantasy, as in the golden monochrome used for the creation of Man), and Adam and Eve look like magazine models.

Once the difficult passages of Creation and the Fall are past, the film is much more sure-footed. The brief, charged episode of Cain and Abel is set, suggestively, in a rocky, volcanic landscape. Richard Harris's Cain has an elemental rage. The Tower of Babel interlude is an art director's triumph, the twisted, soaring tower looming ominously above

an unyielding desert. The sequence concludes with a series of stunning high-angle long shots of the disperal of the twelve tribes.

The Noah's Ark episode has an appealing rustic humour. Noah is an absent-minded oaf, his wife is a shrew, and the two squabble without pause. The procession of the animals, two-by-two, is filmed from a long shot which places the side of the ark in the right corner of the frame. It is a lyrical and touching moment.

The longest section, including the story of Abraham, Sarah, and Lot, the destruction of Sodom and Gomorrah, and the sacrifice that tests Abraham's loyalty to God, is beautifully played in a remote, stylised manner that retains the rhythms of Biblical speech. The domestic triangle involving Abraham, Sarah, and Hagar is handled cryptically, and as in the Bible, the characters are observed externally, as participants in a drama that seems deceptively simple. There is never any sense, as in many costume films, that we are seeing a modern scene in curious period clothing. The characters seem distant and exotic, and the stylised aura is heightened by the ornamental, chiaroscuro lighting.

The wickedness of the cities of the plain (which looks like a rehearsal for *Satyricon*) is suggested with restraint. A panning camera picks out half-lit scenes of grotesque sensuality while colours are suppressed to grim shades of brown. The revellers look like surreal images from a nightmare.

The final sequence depicts Abraham and Isaac's walk through a craggy landscape. There is no mention in the Bible of the kind of scenery that Abraham passed on his way to the mountaintop sacrifice, or of what he was thinking; yet it is typical of the film's imaginative expansion of Biblical economy that the landscape serves as an ideal objective correlative to Abraham's tortured state of mind.

The Bible is an intelligent collaboration with sacred text. Like Genesis itself, the film relates its stories elliptically, without underscoring the archetypal significance of their themes. Events of universal import, actions that dramatise elemental human psychology and that portray the founding of the Hebrew nation, are handled with purposeful casualness. Huston's delicate and reserved film, arriving at the end of the epic cycle begun in the Fifties, has not received the critical recognition it deserves.

5. National Epics

National epics have aims as lofty, and as simple, as those of religious epics. Dramatising a crisis in a country's development, national epics are a blend of nostalgia, patriotism, piety, and celebration. Typically set during a period of war or revolution that tests the strength of the tribe or the community or the state, national epics reflect the national spirit through the development of a single character or representative group of characters. *Beowulf, The Song of Roland*, and the poem of *The Cid* are national epics that commemorate glory-seeking heroes who save kingdoms; *War and Peace*, through the fate of a representative family, expresses the national spirit of Russia during a crucial period in its history.

Essential subjects of the American national epic are the American Revolution, the Civil War, and the conquest and settlement of the frontier. In American films, though, as well as in American literature, these large subjects have been surprisingly neglected. American historical figures have been slighted as well. There has been no full-scale biography of a Founding Father, of Washington or Franklin or Jefferson; at best, these national heroes turn up for cameo appearances, as mere window-dressing, in lacklustre films like *The Buccaneer* (1938 and 1958) or *John Paul Jones* (1959). Griffith's *Abraham Lincoln* (1930) is one of the rare efforts to give epic treatment to a central figure in American history. Griffith certainly had the temperament for such a project, but the film, his first in sound, is strangely downbeat and truncated, lacking the demonic energy that propelled his great silent epics. In the opening scene, the camera pans through a dark forest on a stormy night until it comes to rest on an isolated log cabin—a splendid introduction to the story of a man singled out by destiny to lead his country. There are powerful sequences in the film of black road gangs and of slavery auctions that reverse Griffith's racial posture in *The Birth of a Nation* fifteen years before; but these scenes, which have a lyrical power and are as haunting as anything Griffith had accomplished in his heyday, were deleted from the final print. The film is more sympathetic to the Great Emancipator than Griffith's staunch Southern patriotism would have indicated, though finally it is a curiously muted portrait that emanates an aura of the film-maker's own sense of defeat, since by 1930 Griffith was out of favour, an anachronism in the Hollywood he helped to found. *Abraham Lincoln* lacks the authority, the aggressive attack, that animates *The Birth of a Nation*.

Significantly, there was no book or film that could serve as an official mascot for the Bicentennial celebration, and theatres wanting to salute the nation's two hundredth birthday were forced to show

Vassily Lanavoi as Prince Bolkonsky, in the Russian War and Peace, *a film that was intended to be a national monument.*

revivals of *1776*, an undistinguished musical that nonetheless has an appropriately festive and patriotic spirit. There is no single American film made as a national gesture in the way that Abel Gance's *Napoléon* (1927) and Sergei Bondarchuk's *War and Peace* commemorated epochal events in the history of France and Russia. Produced over a period of many years, and at a staggering cost of one hundred million dollars, *War and Peace* was made to enshrine Tolstoy's novel and to affirm the heroic Russian spirit during a crisis. The film has become something of a national monument since it is shown, in four parts, on a continuous basis in a large Moscow theatre. The film is more spectacular than any American-made epic; the sets, the battle scenes, the grand ball, Napoleon's retreat from Moscow, all assault the audience with their immensity. There are high angle long shots of warfare that seem to contain half the population of Russia. As a director of colossal subjects, Bondarchuk is enorm-

ously talented; his handling of masses, his rapid editing and mobile camerawork in the battle sequences, are wonderfully fluent. The war scenes equal those of Griffith and Eisenstein while surpassing them in scale. As a director of intimate moments, Bondarchuk is less secure, and the personal drama is overwhelmed by the film's monumental design. The characters and the philosophical debates are never fully developed (the relative flatness of the foreground story may be partly a result of the metallically dubbed English version). Unlike truly innovative directors of epic themes like Griffith, Eisenstein, Lang, and Pasolini, Bondarchuk has no immediately discernible personal style; his mammoth film does not reflect a personal vision or a specifically national temperament. Bondarchuk synthesises many aspects of conventional epic style: long takes, sedate camerawork, and close-ups for the intimate scenes; complex editing schemes and a whirling, frantic camera for the grand public sections. It is certainly a flawed film, but it is also as "stupendous" and "colossal" as the ads for epic

Two scenes from D. W. Griffith's almost forgotten America, *1924: a tableau of George Washington at Valley Forge; a group of patriots in a log cabin surrounded by Indians and redcoats, in the film's rousing melodramatic finale.*

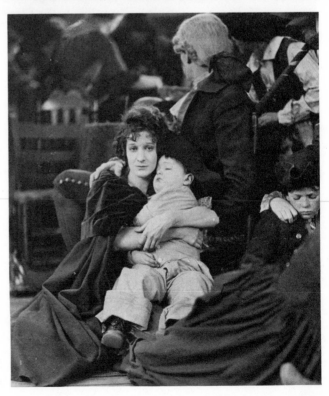

movies always promise. *War and Peace* is an exhilarating spectacle, a gigantic national pageant that outdoes Hollywood, and no American epic has been undertaken in the same spirit of passionate civic pride.

Among potential subjects for epics on American history, the American Revolution has been especially overlooked. The one major film set in the Revolutionary period is Griffith's *America*. The ambitious title, however, is misleading. It has always been recognised that Griffith, an ardent Southerner, was less engaged by the Revolution than by the Civil War; he simply had less feeling about the fight for independence, and the film reflects his relative detachment. Still, *America* deserves a higher reputation than it has, especially since it remains the one epic elaboration of the subject. As in his other films with historical settings, Griffith places in the foreground a group of characters derived from Nineteenth-century stage melodrama: the brave, handsome hero, his high-born mistress whose father is a Tory, the evil British soldier with wild imperialist schemes. Griffith treats the Indians and the British, who are leagued together against the American settlers, the way he presents the blacks in *The Birth of a Nation*, as foreign and corrupting influences that must be expelled in order to maintain what in effect amounts to a kind of racial purity. The film rearranges history; real events, like the clash between American and British soldiers at Concord, and the ride of Paul Revere, brush against the fictional episodes with Indians who are inspired by a deranged British general to attack white settlers. And, as in *The Birth of a Nation*, a historical war is reduced, in the final reel, to a rousing last minute rescue in which an isolated group of rebels is surrounded by Indians and redcoats only to be saved at the climax by a charging cavalry. The American Revolution is thus rendered in the iconography of a standard Western shoot-out.

America is a peculiar reading of history, and the principal characters lack passion, but the film manages nonetheless to suggest sweeping historical forces. Despite its tendency to provincialise American history by viewing the Revolution through the perspective of a Nineteenth-century bigot, the film has scope; and the magnificent battle scenes demonstrate Griffith's continuing skill in cross-cutting and composition. Paul Revere's ride, for which Griffith employs a moving camera and anticipates CinemaScope by masking the top and bottom of the frame to obtain an elongated, horizontal perspective, is the film's visual highpoint. The director's masterful editing astonishingly transforms his primitive historical interpretations into a rousing drama.

Griffith also, of course, made the one substantial film on the Civil War, though *The Birth of a Nation* represents an even greater split than *America* between Griffith's form and content. Propelled by the force of a moral obsession, *The Birth of a Nation* is a blatantly racist tract. Apologists maintain, like Griffith himself, that the film merely reflects historical truth, but the film is in fact a wildly distorted reading of the Reconstruction. Griffith's depiction of blacks is laced with paranoia and hatred, the only blacks who are treated sympathetically being the Uncle Toms, the servants who maintain their loyalty to their white masters. The others, and particularly two mulattoes, are characterised as viciously opportunistic. Both mulatto characters (played by white actors in ghastly stage make-up) are lascivious toward whites, double-dealing, lustful for power. The film presents the black man, in league with conniving Northerners, as determined to destroy the moral order of the South. Preposterously, and dangerously, Griffith enshrines the Ku Klux Klan as the heroic white Southern response to the black threat.

The film's hero, the Little Colonel, devises the idea of the Klan when he sees white children, dressed in sheets, terrifying black children. The scene of his momentous discovery is given an epic setting; he is high on a moutain, overlooking a lush, unpolluted valley, and his plan for Southern salvation is equated in the *mise en scène* to the ennobling beauty of the landscape. The Little Colonel's brainstorm is presented as a visionary's mystical moment, an epiphany that sanctifies white purity.

Another key episode that reflects the director's sentiments is when a big black man attempts to rape the Little Colonel's frail, virginal sister. The scene in which she is chased through the forest by the rampaging black buck and then, in a frenzy, plunges from a mountaintop to her death, has a primal terror. Griffith here shamelessly exploits audience fears of the black man as sexual threat. Later in the film, the theme is reiterated with equal force when the mulatto tyrant attempts to seduce the virginal Northern white heroine (Lillian Gish).

The Birth of a Nation is a powerful statement that always arouses violent reactions since its impact is immediate, relentless, and savage. It portrays as vigorously as any film ever has the effects of war on a settled society. There are images of chaos and decay as the home of the film's representative Southern family is invaded by bands of marauding black soldiers, the Camerons' gracious antebellum way of life shattering before our eyes. The terror of blacks that the film documents is genuine and elemental—Griffith's obsessive pride in the Southern heritage that is challenged by the carpetbaggers, accounts for the film's fierce, manic, insidious energy. *The Birth of a Nation* is, indeed, as Woodrow Wilson claimed, "history written with lightning"; but it is also American history as national nightmare, as racial fears gone wild, exploding in a series of bitter indictments that express Griffith's deep-seated prejudice. (For all its outrageous treatment of blacks, the film is more muted than its source, a novel called *The Klansman* by Thomas Dixon, a vicious piece of propaganda that overflows with overt racial slurs.)

The Birth of a Nation is one of the great paradoxes and embarrassments in American films since its obsessive power transforms Griffith's scurrilous tract into a great movie. Many of the characteristics of the epic film are established here, particularly in the blending of the private drama, involving the Little Colonel's family and the star-crossed lovers, with the public theme. The Camerons' house is an important icon because its changes reflect the disruptions of Southern society. (The family house is a recurrent image in many epics: Tara, in *Gone with the Wind*; the Reata mansion in *Giant*; the Zhivago residence in *Dr. Zhivago* (1965); the imposing family house in *The Magnificent Ambersons* (1942).) *The Birth of a Nation* also sets epic precedent in popularising history by dramatising it through the actions of a group of fictional characters with whom general audiences can readily identify.

With its prologue about the arrival of the black man in America and its unintentionally ironic epilogue in which the horrors of war yield to universal peace and love (as in *Intolerance*), the film vigorously claims for itself a truly epic scope. As in *America*, Griffith's characters seem propelled by historical destiny. Events spiral upward, and fatality stalks the South until the Little Colonel divines the KKK as a miraculous agent of self-defence against black pollution.

The other monumental Civil War film is *Gone with the Wind*. Its treatment of the war is of course much blander than Griffith's pockmarked, ferocious history lesson. *Gone with the Wind* is not interested in rewriting history but in celebrating, in Scarlett O'Hara, particularly American character traits such as resourcefulness, ambition, and independence. *The Birth of a Nation* is an intensely personal work, a sincere reflection of one man's racial and patriotic obsessions, while *Gone with the Wind* is perhaps the supreme example of the Hollywood assembly line method. It is the ultimate factory film, impersonal, finely crafted, shrewdly shaped for popular taste, and therefore, in its greater neutrality, closer in spirit than Griffith's disfigured masterwork to the objective nature of classical epics.

Judged in terms of epic as opposed to popular romance, however, *Gone with the Wind* is seriously flawed. It is the most famous of Hollywood epics and

yet, in crucial ways, it violates *genre* conventions. The film's scope narrows claustrophobically so that the post-intermission segment undercuts the epic sweep and pageantry of the first part. Until the break, the film dutifully observes the traditions of the Hollywood epic format. The herione is carefully framed against a society about to erupt; private and public concerns are beautifully fused as the human drama is enacted against a seething historical background. Part One provides a steady rush of events: the week-end house party, the ball at Atlanta, the burning of the city, and the return to Tara. All these incidents have an epic dimension. When Scarlett and Melanie return through a ravaged Southern landscape to a charred, desolated Tara, the film has completed an epic cycle since the emptied city, the darkened countryside, and the ruined mansion stand in eloquent contrast to the vision of antebellum elegance with which the film opens. But an epic does not end in defeat, and so Scarlett and her society must undergo a period of reconstruction. This part of the drama, however, lacks the density and tension of the war sequences, and therefore the film's overall structure is anticlimactic. The big moments are all contained in the first segment, while the focus of the post-intermission drama becomes progessively narrow, and the film's originally lofty tone plunges downward to shrill melodrama. The spectacular public events leading up to and following upon the Civil War have all been exhausted, leaving only the repetitive personal drama to unravel.

As if preparing for the diminished momentum of the Reconstruction episodes, the director, Victor Fleming, expends his energies on the earlier sections. All the famous shots (with their grandiose camera movements) that seek aggressively to impart epic stature to Scarlett's history, occur in the film's earlier section. The first is when Scarlett's father delivers a hymn to the beauty and the value of the land as the camera retreats from the two characters to frame them in a panoramic perspective. The high-angle long shot of Scarlett and her father standing beneath a cypress, with Tara looming majestically in the background against a vivid sunset, makes a spendid picture. The shot links the personal story to the larger social theme of the Southern heritage. (The impressive fact about the film's first part is that Scarlett seems a big enough character to support the epic framework; she is heroic and important enough to represent through

Scarlett confronts the horrors of war, in one of the most famous scenes in Gone With the Wind.

her own history the charm and instability of antebellum society.) The sentimental but effective long shot of Tara becomes a *leitmotif* throughout Part One, and it is used to end the section on an operatic note as Scarlett, standing firmly on the land, with Tara and a lurid sunset as backdrops, swears to defend her Southern inheritance.

The other celebrated epic image occurs when Scarlett runs to downtown Atlanta to get a doctor to help with the delivery of Melanie's baby. As she races into the town square, covered with bodies of wounded soldiers, the camera, mounted on a crane, rises to an unforgettable high-angle shot of row upon row of recumbent figures, with Scarlett a bewildered, isolated presence in the midst of human suffering. As an image of the horror of war, the shot is one of the most powerful in movies. As a means of integrating the private drama into the large histori-

cal forces that swirl around it, the shot is brilliantly calculated. Like much else in Margaret Mitchell's romantic extravaganza, these big moments, in which the director uses film means to heighten the scale of the drama, are florid and manipulative. But such high points in Part One are in their own way privileged moments that enrich the film's portrait of a society in painful transition.

Part Two has nothing to compare with the pace and colour of the earlier section. Scarlett's private history—her cleverness in surviving, her sharp business sense, her unrequited love for Ashley, her tumultuous and ill-fated marriage to Rhett Butler, the death of her child, the death of Ashley, the final separation with Rhett, the final return to Tara—is glossy, old-fashioned romance. From a truly epic presentation of a society, the film narrows its focus to a series of purely private catastrophes, its scale drastically reduced to that of a ladies' magazine

The ultimate Western hero: Alan Ladd as Shane, 1952.

tearjerker. The major dramatic event of Part Two occurs when Ashley, Rhett and friends attempt to avenge Scarlett's attack by a group of black renegades. The women wait tensely as the men risk their lives on a mission of vengeance. Since the event is not genuinely significant, the high drama of the sequence looks altogether manufactured.

Though outrageously spoiled, Scarlett is a resourceful, energetic heroine, and generations of moviegoers have responded warmly to Vivien Leigh's exquisite performance. Scarlett embodies the spirit of a deeply wounded South attempting to resurrect itself; but her heroic mission is undercut by the film's melodramatic excess in which personal misfortune cancels the larger theme of Southern Reconstruction. Vivien Leigh certainly plays with the stature befitting an epic heroine, but ultimately the film fails as an epic of Southern history.

★

The frontier setting has been used in many films, though seldom with epic significance. The themes of frontier settlement and of manifest destiny have supplied background texture for many westerns, most prominently those of John Ford and isolated, ambitious westerns like Howard Hawks's *Red River* (1948). Westerns on an epic scale are rare, however, and there is no one large-scale western that fully elaborates the pioneer theme. For the most part, the western is comfortable on a smaller canvas. Many of the famous westerns (like *High Noon*, 1952, and *The Gunfighter*, 1950) are in fact intimate in focus. Most westerns release their larger meanings through a relatively restricted foreground, a private drama not conceived on a heroic scale. All westerns deal with myths about the frontier and the cowboy, but few raise the myths to an epic level. Sometimes, in fact, the attempt to present a western theme on a grand scale only diminishes the unpretentious quality that has been the continuing appeal of the western format. Westerns, then, have proven serviceable for modest action films as well as dense political and psychological allegories, but have seldom been hospitable to epic amplitude.

Three westerns planned for monumental effect—*Duel in the Sun, Shane,* and *The Big Country*—tamper with generic formulas in ways that are strained and inorganic. These big films are not "pure" westerns, and no *aficionado* would list them as among his favourites. As Robert Warshow suggests in his famous essay on "The Westerner," *Shane* attempts to be the ultimate western. The film raises a standard land battle between ranchers and farmers to the heights of legend. Events of modest and limited significance, and character types familiar from routine westerns, are treated as luminous archetypes. Every action in the film is underlined for its mythic potential. Shane, dressed in gleaming white, materialises out of the hills as if by magic in order to do battle against the villain, dressed in ceremonial black. The ensuing battle between good and evil is handled with ritualistic decorum and with a controlled visual elegance that is meant to dignify stereotype. Coming from the hills and then returning to them after he has cleansed the valley of the corrupt ranchers, Shane is like a questing medieval knight, supremely gallant and valorous, who brings to the Western setting a concept of chivalry inherited from Arthurian romance. He is impossibly pure and noble (even if he is a man of violence), and the film tries to counter the exaggerated characterisation by presenting the hero from the point of view of a child: the idea is that we are seeing an innocent child's version of a saviour.

George Stevens's poetic direction is marked by his lush and unspoiled landscapes; by his elegantly tracking camera; and his generous use of a romantic score. As Warshow notes, *Shane* is made as if it were the last western since it pushes generic elements to the breaking point. For all its studied beauty, however, *Shane* is one of the few sustained attempts in American films to treat western *motifs* in an epic framework, as the raw material for a national fable; in it, the cowboy becomes an American counterpart to Beowulf, a magnetic and divinely favoured hero who cleanses the land of evil.

Epic treatments of the west enhance two silent films, *The Covered Wagon* and *The Iron Horse,* which was the prototype for DeMille's *Union Pacific* (1939). Both films deal with subjects ideally suited to a visual medium: the westward journey of the pioneers, and the construction of the transcontinental railroad. Both movies reinforce their big subjects with long shots of covered wagons making their way through a panoramic landscape and of rows of coolies laying the iron crossbars for the train that will transport Eastern civilisation to the Western wilderness. Both films, cluttered with *papier-mâché* characters and dime-novel romantic triangles, nevertheless transcend the impoverished personal drama by celebrating the heroism of the pioneers and of the railroad workers, and by enshrining native values of courage, endurance, and farsightedness.

The Covered Wagon, the first large-scale western, has elements that were visual *clichés* even in 1923: the Indian attack, the cavalry rescue, the hazardous crossing of the river, the buffalo stampede; and yet the impact of the film is more forceful than its routine elements would suggest. Silence both universalises and elevates the traditional obstacles that confront the pioneers, and the "journey" format achieves an archetypal significance.

The trek, the journey, and the quest provide the framework for many westerns, of course, but these patterns seldom have monumental impact. John Ford's one sound western clearly designed in an epic mould is *Cheyenne Autumn.* The film is made in a spirit of commemoration as it records the heroic journey of the Cheyennes on a defiant return to the reservation from which they have been expelled. Beautifully filmed in Ford's beloved Monument Valley, *Cheyenne Autumn* has a melancholy tone unusual for epic themes. Mixing epic elements with strains of lyric and elegy, the film, in fact, is curiously staid. Ford is clearly happier in a smaller-scale project like *Stagecoach,* in which his style is much more expressive. It may be that Ford felt inhibited by the scope as well as the solemn theme of *Cheyenne Autumn,* and that its epic trappings encouraged him to emphasise external compositional elements rather than personal drama. The film, at any rate, lacks the high spirits of Ford's earlier westerns.

Stagecoach has loosely been described as an epic, but it does not really qualify. Though its story is told in the form of a journey, and though it has a saviour-like hero and an epic treatment of landscape, the film does not possess a large theme. *Stagecoach* is a collection of potboiler *clichés* redeemed by superior acting and by Ford's exhilarating direction, with its striking use of chiaroscuro, its

Richard Widmark and Carroll Baker in a quiet moment from John Ford's self-consciously epic Western, Cheyenne Autumn, *1964.*

seductively panning camera, its rousing comedy and climactic Indian attack.

The Searchers also has the superficial form of an epic—a quest set against spectacular vistas—but the theme is too purely private in focus to qualify the film as an American epic. But in *The Searchers*, as in *Stagecoach*, Ford's direction is wonderfully fluent and expansive, whereas in *Cheyenne Autumn*, Ford seems intimidated by his high theme, which many critics felt represented the director's attempt to atone for his unsympathetic treatment of Indians in several of his earlier westerns. Conscious of working on a revisionist approach to his own mythic interpretations of the West, Ford directs in a stiff and declamatory style; and the journey *motif* lacks the emotional quality of the odyssey of those other dispossessed Americans in Ford's exquisite *The Grapes of Wrath* (1940). The impoverished characters are closely observed, and their passage from Oklahoma to California assumes thematic significance while retaining its human scale. Characterisation is not sacrificed for rhetoric, as it is in *Cheyenne Autumn*, where the Indians are merely icons in a kind of national pageant—handsome figures placed picturesquely against stunning panoramas.

The Grapes of Wrath has an epic rhythm that is only partially achieved in *Cheyenne Autumn*, and despite Ford's studied use of chiaroscuro, the film never falls into the artificial style that mars the later film. *The Grapes of Wrath* has an authentic tone, and though it considerably softens the political point of view of John Steinbeck's novel, it doesn't condescend to its characters, or deny their gross mistreatment by the government. Despite its sentimental blurring of issues, the film is one of the few socially engaged American epics, a large-scale work that employs an epic structure to launch an indictment against the status quo.

★

87

Doris Bowden, Jane Darwell, and Henry Fonda as the dispossessed farmers, in John Ford's The Grapes of Wrath, *1940.*

One film that could have been a true national epic, because of its enormous scope, was *How the West Was Won*. With its three veteran directors noted for their contributions to the western (George Marshall, Henry Hathaway, and Ford), its vast framework that includes every aspect of the taming of the West, and its Cinerama screen, the film could have been a glorious national pageant. As it traces the movement of a pioneer family in its zigzagging cross-country trek, the film covers a great sweep of American history. In prospect, the fertile subject matter and the giant screen seemed an ideal pairing, but the screenplay reduces the quintessentially American tapestry to a comic book level. The rambling script features a procession of incidents too insignificant to dramatise adequately the experience of the pioneers, and the rich chronicle of America's westward expansion is scaled down to a series of western movie *clichés* (as trite as the

formulaic elements of *Stagecoach*) and a parade of spectacular effects. Three of the big scenes epitomise the technological expertise of the special effects department: the family's battle with the raging river; the buffalo stampede; and the shoot-out on the train. All three beautifully edited sequences make full use of the Cinerama screen, and the fluid compositions avoid the static quality that afflicted the CinemaScope movies of the early Fifties.

But no matter how magnificently handled these episodes are, they are no more than exciting set pieces because they are not anchored in a convincing dramatic context. The pioneers' westward odyssèy is prettified for mass consumption, and it is no accident that the film's most prominent pioneer, its representative questing American, is Debbie Reynolds—resourceful yet hopelessly bland. Experience hardly touches her, and that is perhaps the secret of her survival; from pioneer daughter to dance-hall hostess to successful entrepreneur, she is a vindication of the self-contained capitalistic spirit, reacting to reversals and triumphs in the same detached manner. Her character survives to a respectable old age because she remains immune to her surroundings. The vapid, fun-loving Reynolds character, who remains fundamentally unserious in the face of experiences of potentially monumental significance, sets the film's glossy tone.

How the West Was Won has a greater scope than any other Western. It covers more space and more time, it has more characters and incidents, and yet its dimensions, finally, seem very limited. It is a provincial treatment of a national theme. As an epic enactment of a pioneer drama, Elia Kazan's *America, America* (1963) and Jan Troell's *The Emigrants* (1972) and *The New Land* (1974) have the intensity that the Cinerama extravaganza so fearfully lacks. Kazan's depiction of a Greek peasant's embattled passage to America and Troell's two-part chronicle of the journey to the new world of dispossessed Swedish emigrants are passionate works. These epic

voyages are filled with suffering, physical anguish, fierce battles with man and nature. The pioneers in these films are not idealised figures, but flesh-and-blood characters who are forced to compromise their values in order to reach America. The sea voyage in *The Emigrants* and the combat with Indians in *The New Land* are unsparingly violent. Unlike the antiseptic *How the West Was Won*, Kazan's and Troell's visceral epics force the audience to experience the hardships of the pioneers and to admire their tenacity. These are the most impassioned statements of the pioneer theme on film.

Less flavourful, but successful epic films have been built on variations of the pioneer saga. *Exodus* (1960) and *Hawaii* (1967) both dramatise the pioneer spirit against an epic canvas—the creation of Israel and the colonisation of Hawaii. In both these underrated movies, the private drama is closely governed by public events, since large concepts like historical destiny and heroic en-

On board the Exodus, *in Otto Preminger's pioneer epic, 1960.*

Max von Sydow as an obsessed minister in another pioneer epic, Hawaii, *1966.*

ment or the imaginative grasp to realise it fully. But Max von Sydow's characterisation of a possessed minister who brutally enforces his Calvinist doctrines on the resistant, alien culture of the native Hawaiians, is remarkably intense. Only after his wife dies and he loses his parish is the minister chastened; and purified by madness, he becomes a holy recluse, a kind of local talisman. Von Sydow's complex, driven character, so deeply unsuited to his missionary goals, is an unusual hero for an epic, and the film has the integrity not to romanticise him. Coming at the end of the epic cycle, and unevenly edited, the film nonetheless has more impact than its meagre reputation suggests.

★

Like the westerner, the gangster, another archetypal American hero, is also best suited to modest *genre* films. The gangster cycle in the Thirties, like the western cycle in the Fifties, functioned best at an unself-conscious level, treating formulaic elements in a direct and uninflated style. The trim, hard-boiled manner was a sign, in fact, of the films' authenticity; the gangster movies were in a sense contemporary documents, paralleling newspaper headlines. Like the westerns, the gangster films could yield meanings on several levels at once—as journalistic reportage, as disguised vindications of American values of power and material success, as moral tracts. But the films were popular because they were fast action entertainments about, as Robert Warshow wrote, "men who use guns."

The first and only gangster epic, Francis Ford Coppola's *The Godfather*, does for the gangster movie what *Shane* did for the western: it builds an elaborate structure over traditional *genre* elements. The film is slowed down to a stately, princely rhythm; it's as if Coppola, like George Stevens, is presenting a classic American story for the last time, since his is the most sophisticated version of the gangster legend, the most intellectually and artistically self-aware.

The two parts of *The Godfather* provide a complex epic structure. Like classical epics, the film begins *in media re*. Part Two, which supplies details of the early manhood of the godfather, deepens the family history that was introduced in Part One. The story of the Corleones describes the clash between two cultures as the Sicilian family founded by Don

deavour in the founding of a nation, qualify the actions of the characters. The swirling historical backgrounds help to define character.

Exodus places its characters in a dynamic relationship to epochal events. The chaos that culminates in the partition of Palestine offers a powerful subject for which Otto Preminger's characteristic tracking shots and craning, roving camera are well-suited. As befits a modern epic, the performances are pitched in a cool, naturalistic key; and Preminger maintains the objectivity of classical epic by telling the story largely from the point of view of an outsider, an American Gentile (Eva Marie Saint) who is only gradually drawn to the Jewish cause. (*Exodus* is a latter-day Story of Ruth.) The character's initial distance from the drama allows us to perceive the historical events in broad outline.

The exploitation of Hawaii by zealous European missionaries is another enormous subject, and George Roy Hill's film does not have the tempera-

Corleone becomes assimilated to the New World and establishes for itself a prominent place in the Mafia. The film deals with several themes that have epic scope, since the family's history contains a saga of immigration and provides as well a microcosmic view of the development of the American underworld.

In more incisive ways than the cycle of gangster stories in the Thirties, *The Godfather* probes the psychology of the gangster. The development of Michael Corleone from innocent to reptilian criminal is one of the most complete presentations in American films of the making of a gangster. Michael is the cold-eyed anti-hero of a dark American epic, a story of the American Mafia which, with its regimen of codes and its social hierarchy, is as stratified and as tightly woven as the society in Homer. The dense social fabric helps to give the two-part film its truly epic stature. The underworld society that the film documents so meticulously has the stable, cere-

monious quality of life that permeates traditional epics like *The Iliad, Beowulf, The Cid,* and *The Song of Roland. The Godfather* is about the founding of a regulated, deeply self-protective community. Part Two links the patterns of community behaviour in the present to those in the Old World and in the melting pot of the Lower East Side. The system of obligations and demands, the patterns of revenge and reprisal, are as complex, as rigorously codified, as those in a courtly medieval or ancient society.

The evolutionary pattern traced by *The Godfather*—the founding and development, over a long period of time, of a way of life, a social and national consciousness—is a standard epic construct, and one particularly suited to films (as well as to best-selling novels by writers like Edna Ferber and James Michener). The best of the American films built on the pattern of social evolution is George

The gangster saga raised to epic heights: Marlon Brando as The Godfather, 1972.

Exquisite Wellesian mise-en-scène: *Agnes Moorehead and Tim Holt on the famous staircase, in* The Magnificent Ambersons, *1942.*

Stevens's *Giant,* in which Texas, like the underworld in *The Godfather,* is developed as a subject with national overtones. The film sets up a contrast between two kinds of wealth, inherited money and that which is newly-won. Beyond that is the clash between two ways of life, the rural, structured, feudalistic style of the Benedicts, perfectly symbolised by the Victorian Gothic mansion that dominates their Reata Ranch with such grim authority, and the paranoid *nouveau riche* aggressiveness represented by Jett Rink (James Dean), who discovers oil on his land, and who becomes progressively unhinged from making too much money. As befits an epic on the growth of the American character from rural to urban, *Giant* is about the corrosive power of money.

Décor is extremely important in suggesting not only the passage of time, but also shifts in sensibility and taste and in the organisation of society. The isolated mansion in the film's early sections, with its rich, heavy furnishings, makes a pointed contrast to the antiseptic modern hotel at the end, and the change in architecture seems to contain a lament for the older, more ordered way of life. The nostalgic note is present in the film's pacing, since the opening has a graceful, flowing movement while the conclusion in the hotel, with crowded frames and hectic intercutting, is purposefully chaotic.

Giant is a mediocre novel that makes colourful but superficial points about Texas. The film, with its more immediate impact and its powerfully composed images, is a much more evocative treatment of Texas as a microcosm of the American thrust toward wealth and urbanisation. Other Edna Ferber novels with the same kind of evolutionary structure (*Cimarron, Ice Palace*) were less successful in their adaptation to film. Again, Ferber's overblown structure proved congenial to film's fluid handling of time, but the settings had less symbolic force than in Stevens's exquisite film, and the characterisations were not as resonant as those in *Giant*. The Benedict family in *Giant* is as potent a representative of American values as the Corleone clan in *The Godfather*.

Like *Giant*, Orson Welles's *The Magnificent Ambersons* (1942) also suggests powerfully the passage from one style of life to another. Welles's film too records the passing of an American era, and like Stevens's movie it looks nostalgically at the rural America that is progressively coarsened and disrupted by technology (the automobile here, as opposed to oil in *Giant*) and subsequent shift to the cities. Though its scope and theme have magnitude, *The Magnificent Ambersons* is more lyric and elegy than it is epic. The social background is etched with remarkable economy, as a series of footnotes to the private drama about mothers and sons, fathers and daughters, and unconsummated romances. Ele-

gantly photographed, with many celebrated compositions in depth and shadow, with settings that comment sharply on the decline of the "magnificent" Amberson family, and superbly acted in the distinctive Wellesian mode of stylised naturalism, *The Magnificent Ambersons* is a lament for a vanished America. In tone as well as social notation, there is nothing else quite like it in American films.

Because he has always had to struggle with severe financial restrictions, Welles has never been able to make the full-scale epic that his grandiose, theatrical temperament is drawn toward. Even with shoe-string budgets, the scenes of public ceremony in *Macbeth* and the battle scenes in *Falstaff* have a remarkable texture. *Ambersons* was cut by RKO, yet this mutilated version has a rare visual and emotional grandeur. Though it does not treat its large subject in a traditional epic manner, being deliberately restricted in scale and settings, it is nevertheless an evocative portrait of a wrenching shift in national style and sensibility.

6. Historical Epics

Historical epics that have neither a religious nor a nationalist theme are a problematic *genre*. Unable to depend on the appeal of religious and patriotic *motifs*, these films must seek other means of connecting to audiences and of establishing some contemporary relevance. Films like *The Egyptian, Land of the Pharaohs, Alexander the Great, Helen of Troy, Spartacus, Cleopatra,* and *The Fall of the Roman Empire*, with pre-Christian, Egyptian, Greek, and Roman settings, are understandably rare. To interest audiences, the films must have some aim beyond their recreation of an ancient world. Their lavish sets, their pageantry, their exotic appeal, their use of history, must be purposeful, the films' *raison d'être* the definition of heroism or the underlining of a pertinent historical idea.

A pre-Christian costume epic like *The Egyptian*, for instance, clearly has trouble in knowing how to use the past creatively and with contemporary impact. The film-makers try to transform pagan Egypt into a semblance of early Christian Rome, and the film's ennobling theme becomes Pharaoh Akhnaton's belief in One God. The conflict the film establishes between believers and infidels had comfortable parallels to the Biblical spectacles being made at the same time. Akhnaton's followers, who wear an emblem and who are slaughtered by Pharaoh's soldiers, are thus iconographically re-lated to the persecuted Christians in other early Fifties' films like *Quo Vadis?* and *The Robe*. Akhnaton is presented as a saintly character surrounded by a halo of sunlight in moments of spiritual transfiguration; and the wandering hero, a physician without a country whose wife is killed for her belief in the One God, finds peace finally by embracing Akhnaton's faith. The film artifically attaches to its disjointed narrative the thematic significance associated with Christian drama. On that level, as a drama of religious faith and persecution, it attains a modest power.

The besetting problem with *Cleopatra* is that it never does know exactly what to do with the history it dramatises. The film never carves out a theme large enough to justify its dazzling sets and costumes and its unprecedented expense. A conflation of the events covered by Shaw in *Ceasar and Cleopatra* and by Shakespeare in *Antony and Cleopatra*, the film is essentially schizophrenic as it hovers uncertainly between the small high comedy of the first part and the romantic tragedy of the second. Shaw's play about Caesar has a markedly different intent and tone from Shakespeare's treatment of Antony; and the film reflects the tonal disparities without reconciling them. The result is four hours in which the characters are stranded in search of an epic theme.

Shaw used the Caesar-Cleopatra *contretemps* to

*Borrowing iconography from the Christian epics: worshipers
of the One God under attack, in The Egyptian, 1954.*

Characters in search of an epic theme: Richard Burton and Elizabeth Taylor, in Cleopatra, *1963.*

Laurence Olivier inspects a group of new slaves, in Spartacus, *1960, one of the few explicitly political epics made in Hollywood.*

deflate legendary historical figures; and his play is filled with contemporary references and diction that are designed to puncture the characters' mythic stature. It is a small-scale play, a lightweight romantic comedy built on the Pygmalion-Galatea model of a paternal figure educating and falling in love with an inexperienced girl. *Ceasar and Cleopatra* was not written as a historical spectacle peopled with remote, larger-than-life characters but as a wry history lesson about leadership. The Gabriel Pascal film (1945) with Vivien Leigh and Claude Rains mistook Shaw by turning his trim comedy into a lavish spectacle. The Shavian wit is overshadowed by the elaborate physical production. The full cast of thousands treatment, the towering sets, the full-scale battle scenes, and the gala processions, intrude fatally onto the personal rela-

tionship between a sly, knowing, aging Caesar and a kittenish, shrewd young Queen.

The spectacle in Mankiewicz's version is similarly unnecessary. Rex Harrison and Elizabeth Taylor perform together charmingly, when the script gives them the chance, but the small points of characterisation and of history revealed by their romance are blunted by the urgency of showing off the forty million dollar budget.

The Antony and Cleopatra relationship is less successfully written and played. Yet the filmmakers were clearly counting on the timeless appeal of a doomed romance as their safest bet, as the reason why the property seemed commercial in the first place. The characters are bereft, however, because the historical background is not closely woven enough, and the romantic theme is not sufficiently powerful, to warrant the stupendous production values. Though it violates epic convention by ending in defeat, *Cleopatra* has epic insignia

97

of length, scope, and spectacle, but it fails, ultimately, because it never identifies a unifying and significant historical theme.

Spartacus, on the other hand, is very sharply pointed. It is one of the few epics that does not rely on the religious big time for its impact and that nonetheless dramatises a theme. that both justifies the monumental production and that has contemporary significance as well. The film, which uses ancient history to make a political statement, is one of the rare American epics that has an enlightened political perspective. Powerful epics made abroad, like *Battleship Potemkin* and *The Triumph of the Will*, are clear-cut propaganda, made to enforce a particular ideology. Both films pretend to be objective—*Potemkin*, a faithful historical reconstruction; *Triumph*, a document of history in the making. But both cunningly use editing and camera placement to rearrange and heighten historical reality. Shrewdly and manipulatively edited to achieve maximum dramatic impact, both films are epic in scale.

There is no precise equivalent in American films to Eisenstein's and Riefenstahl's use of the epic mode to indoctrinate audiences. The two films that come closest to the propagandistic flair of the Russian and German film-makers are probably *The Birth of a Nation* (racist propaganda) and *Spartacus*, which, in a more muted way than Griffith's infuriating masterwork, is political propaganda. Written by the blacklisted Dalton Trumbo, the film is a populist epic in which the rebel slave Spartacus is a leader of the people whose political ideas are directly opposed to the decadent leadership of the Roman Senate and in particular of the effete aristocrat, Crassus. The film does not conceal its leftist sympathies, its excited belief in "the people," and as a result the rebel camp is presented sympathetically as a kind of proto-communist society with work and family chores shared among its members. Built on a contrast that is sustained through continuous crosscutting, the film pivots the equalitarian rebel slaves against the corrupt Roman government.

One sequence in particular enforces the political parallel. Before the climactic battle between Spartacus's ragged army and the Roman legions, the film cuts back and forth between Spartacus's and Crassus's speeches to their followers. Spartacus's speech is direct, rough-hewn, plain-spoken, while Crassus speaks in the elegant, slippery style of a practiced rhetorician. The casting shrewdly underscores the political point since Kirk Douglas speaks in an unaffected, energetic American manner while Laurence Olivier intones his oration in glorious English diction.

The film makes palpable the hatred of the masses for a corrupt dictatorial government that treats its lowly subjects like items on a menu. There is a strong scene, early in the film, in which a group of decadent patricians visits a gladiatorial training school, and with extravagant indifference, selects two men to entertain them by fighting to the death. The people's grievances are thus directly portrayed, with the immediacy possible in films. The film depicts its political sympathies and antipathies broadly, its revolutionary fervour remaining surprisingly direct. Though Spartacus loses, the film presents him as victorious in defeat, dying Christ-like on a cross. And he has a child who will remember and continue his courageous fight for freedom.

Some historical epics define their purpose by being revisionist and sceptical, and by introducing comic elements to undercut epic pomposity. In his preface to *Joseph Andrews*, Henry Fielding describes his novel as a mock epic in prose—a comic epic. Comedy and the epic form are usually antithetical, the tone of most epics being relentlessly solemn and high-minded. Critics have usually assumed that comic relief can serve only to satirise the exalted purpose of the epic framework. Though they end in triumph, epics are closer in spirit to tragedy and to lyric than to comedy. Some critics, including E.M.W. Tillyard, do not take seriously Fielding's claim to having written a comic epic, and maintain that *Joseph Andrews* and *Tom Jones* are distinctly picaresque as opposed to epic.

Tony Richardson's film of *Tom Jones* (1963) retains the novel's wonderfully robust and sensual surface. Significantly, it has none of the traces of the epic film, its circumference being too small, its protagonist inescapably lightweight, too charming and wicked to qualify as an epic hero. *Tom Jones* is about the moral education of its title character, and its serious insights on human nature are concealed beneath a surface of comic bravado, a fusillage of wit, innuendo, and irony. The thematic focus is purely private since Tom's personal fortunes are not linked to those of country or religion.

Yet Richardson's similar, light-fingered comic technique in *The Charge of the Light Brigade* (1967) does not detract from the epic thrust of the material, but becomes in fact part of its epic texture. It, along with Arthur Penn's *Little Big Man* and, to a lesser extent, Richard Lester's *Robin and Marian*, is a revisionist epic that attempts to correct traditional movie approaches to lofty historical subjects.

The Charge of the Light Brigade has been made almost as if to disprove the jingoism of the earlier Michael Curtiz version (1936), in which the charge is presented as a testament to the heroism of the soldiers who are fighting against impossible odds. Combat in the earlier film is glorified as an occasion for supreme heroism. The picture assumes shared loyalties among its audience. The film accepts without qualification such traditional values as patriotism, the necessity of war, and the belief in imperialism. Like Oliver's *Henry V*, it employs an epic format to celebrate the sanctity of war. Richardson's film has an entirely different point of view (as well as a new story line), though it too concludes with the same disastrous charge of the light brigade. Here, an epic canvas is used for subversive intent. War is presented in the mock-heroic style described by Fielding. In keeping with the anti-war sentiments prevalent at the time the film was made, Richardson presents the charge as a display of monumental human folly, as an index of the imperialist mentality gone berserk. Lord Raglan is portrayed as a foppish buffoon and the film pitilessly reveals the British officers as a group of clowns whose irresponsibility results in massive slaughter. The film audaciously mingles farce and tragedy; laughter sticks in our throats as the camera lingers over the bodies of the dead, the buzz of flies a grim accompaniment to the apocalyptic images.

This updated version of *The Charge of the Light Brigade* is a powerful indictment of the military mentality and mindless patriotism. A fierce criticism of national policies, it is one of the rare radical epics. Richardson tries for daring juxtapositions of mood and tone, from lyrical romantic interludes to scenes of brilliant social comedy to slapstick to final tragedy. The film doesn't lull audiences, or move in the solemn, predictable manner that characterises many epics. Unlike traditional epics, it challenges and condemns community values. This is an epic in the modern spirit, irreverent and profane, and bitterly scornful of the notion that heroism is attainable through combat.

Richardson uses cartoon figures as a *leitmotif* in an effort to undercut the tendency of film to turn warfare into stirring spectacle. Ironically, however, this savage anti-war statement contains some extraordinary military choreography. The war scenes are punctuated with panoramic long shots of columns of soldiers and dynamic cutting in the Eisenstein manner. The sheer sensuous delight of the images threatens to override the debunking theme; Richardson's means are almost too ample for his bitter, mocking intent, and the joyously decorative quality of the *mise en scène* wars with the austere moral purpose.

Like Richardson, Arthur Penn in *Little Big Man* is interested in re-writing conservative versions of history. His General Custer is as befuddled and as vicious as Richardson's concept of Lord Raglan. Custer's incompetence results in the same wholesale slaughter. Like *The Charge of the Light Brigade*, the film works up to a monumental battle (Big Horn) which becomes a focal point for the revisionist theme. The American military figures are presented as bunglers and mad imperialists callously exploiting Indian territory. The battle scene contains the same contradictory elements as in Richardson's film. Visual grandeur and political satire mix in uneasy alliance. The sequence is beautifully filmed in a snow-covered landscape. Custer capers about on the battlefield like a demented child, a knockabout vaudevillian, while all around him his men are being killed. Horror brushes farce in startling counterpoint. As in *Bonnie and Clyde*, made several years ealier, Penn is interested in exploring sharp juxtapositions of mood by mixing wild comedy with extreme violence. The film punctures the usually formal nature of epics with comic interludes ranging from farce and slapstick to a more delicate romantic irony. Dustin Hoffman's performance is curious. Playing a white boy raised by Indians who is forced by destiny into being a hero, Hoffman is deliberately anachronistic. He's hip and knowing in modern city ways that deflate the romantic aura of mythic Western characters played by actors like Gary Cooper and Alan Ladd. Speaking in his usual nasal twang, Dustin Hoffman is a *shlemiel* in the Old West, a sweet quiet guy who resists the traditional heroic posture. Little Big Man, as he is called, learns to shoot and hunt, but he is at heart an unregenerate pacifist in love with the land and with his wise Indian father rather than the Western rituals of combat and self-defence. He is an altogether new kind of hero, appropriate for a revisionist version of American history, and Penn plays on the contradictions to

Stunning juxtapositions of long shot and close-up, in Tony Richardson's The Charge of the Light Brigade, *1968, a radical revision of movie heroism. The film's fierce anti-militarism provides sharp contrast to the many epic films, like Olivier's* Henry V, *1943, that glorify war.*

Dustin Hoffman as the anti-hero in Arthur Penn's revisionist Western, Little Big Man, *1971.*

enforce his anti-war theme and his interest in slashing the myths of the Old West.

Like *The Charge of the Light Brigade, Little Big Man* is a comic didactic epic that introduces a modern sensibility into familiar right wing themes of military glory and patriotism. Both films thrive on their Brechtian use of alienation and dislocation, and both suggest that the epic mode is elastic, capable of being adapted to films in novel ways. These films prove that epics can be audacious and subversive rather than, inevitably, staid official statements about religion, war, and country.

7. The Epic Hero

The first major epic hero in American films is female—D. W. Griffith's *Judith of Bethulia* (1913). Judith saves her people by offering herself to Holofernes, the conqueror whose army is encamped outside the city walls. Judith is a reluctant saviour. Recently widowed, she remains cloistered in her house until the city is threatened and she is called, as if by divine authority, to become a deliverer. Divided between her private loyalties and her sense of civic responsibility, she prays for guidance. Tormented and regal, she is clearly a figure predestined to achieve greatness; she is a special person chosen by fate to rescue her people, and yet she herself must choose to act. After she performs her duty, by entering Holofernes's tent under the guise of giving herself to him, and then decapitating him, she is transformed into a kind of magical, talismanic personage before whom the people of the city bow down in worship. Once having embraced her fate, Judith is free to return to her private life behind bolted doors.

Judith is an archetypal epic hero, since her actions help to shape national destiny. Like the heroes of classical epics, she is aided and inspired by divine powers; she is a chosen one impelled by fate, or by some unspecified transcendental force, to influence the course of history. Like other great saviours in epic films, she is observed largely from the outside. We see her in close-up—Griffith's camera probes her face the way Dreyer's explores Falconetti's as Joan of Arc; and we see her in long shot, as the dominant focus in crowd scenes; but, framed by the mysterious and the ineffable, she is finally an unknowable figure, an icon in a painting. Greater than herself, embodying extraordinary energy, she creates and controls history.

Judith of Bethulia is technically crude. The battle scenes, the settings, the depictions of pagan revelry and of Judaic piety, are naïve, preliminary sketches for the grandeur Griffith achieved three years later in *Intolerance*. But the film's concept of the epic hero is amazingly mature, and Blanche Sweet's performance has a radiant intensity that is seldom matched in later full-scale epics. Her portrayal of movies' first heroic figure has stature and exaltation.

The epic-hero-as-saviour, then, is a spiritual, remote figure whose extraordinary qualities are enhanced by such visual resources as lighting, gesture, and composition. Epic heroes of this kind are presented in a stylised manner whose basic motifs are announced, tentatively, in *Judith of Bethulia,* and in a more formal way in the Christ episodes of *Intolerance,* where Jesus is framed by a halo as He stands at the centre of symmetrical groupings or else occupies the frame alone, separated by editing from the other characters. The magisterial gestures of Griffith's Christ are careful signals of His holiness. Christ is the preeminent epic hero as Saviour, and His presence automatically inspires an elevated style, one that is self-consciously stately and processional. Hollywood depictions of Christ are based on the traditional iconography of Renaissance paintings, and the actors who have portrayed Him suppress emotion and simplify gesture, movement, and speech. The spare, almost abstract approach is intended to soothe mass audiences. American movies have been reluctant to probe or "interpret" Christ, settling instead for displaying Him in a series of exquisitely mounted *tableaux vivants* whose simplicity is often in sharp contrast to the sprawling epic machinery that surrounds the Holy figure. This external presentation forces the actors to function as models who have been selected for their sculpturesque qualities.

Only Max von Sydow's Christ in *The Greatest Story Even Told* has more than emblematic or ornamental significance. With his searching eyes, his lean face and his sombre, beautifully modulated voice, von Sydow makes Christ a figure of depth whose serenity is edged with dark hints of self-doubt, harshness, and spiritual torment. His complex, subtly shaded performance, which attains genuine nobility, has never been fully appreciated.

Pasolini's conception of Christ in *The Gospel According to St. Matthew* has the interpretive daring that the big budget Hollywood films have been unable to attempt. Pasolini re-evaluates the concept of the Holy epic hero. His fiercely messianic Christ is a political as well as a spiritual leader, an unyielding, unsmiling figure more secular than divine. Unwashed, homely, even faintly sexual, Pasolini's revisionist Christ harangues the multitudes whereas the Hollywood Christs speak gently to their followers. There is no softness or forgiveness in Pasolini's fiery political orator. Unlike the American versions, this audacious Christ is not an immaculate spiritual hero but a struggling, imperfect, self-styled messiah with Machiavellian overtones.

Christ is the ultimate hero of the Western tradition, and His story, with its themes of persecution and salvation, of defeat and triumph, is an archetypal epic. The historical Jesus was surely a revolutionary with great reserves of manic drive and energy, but since He has passed from history to legend, He is typically presented as a passive hero touched by divine grace. As Hollywood has traditionally interpreted Him, Christ is not an ideal film hero because he is not portrayed as a man of action but as a teacher and philosopher, and the films with Christ as protagonist are inescapably sedate and declamatory. Their stately pacing gives them amplitude, but epic rhythm requires speed and physical action as well. Ulysses, after all, is the hero of one of the world's great epics, and Ulysses achieves his heroism through driving action and movement. Restless, impulsive, physical heroes are more congenial to films (and, in particular, to the special temperament of Hollywood films) than spiritual heroes. Therefore, worldly heroes and dynamic leaders like Moses, Spartacus, Alexander the Great, El Cid, Lawrence of Arabia, Shane, Henry V, and Alexander Nevsky are more suitable movie characters than Christ. The treatment of Christ in a secular medium like film will always risk sacrilege; except in the rarefied work of directors like Bresson and Ozu, films which are rooted in a specific time and place are hostile to the depiction of divinity and transcendence. The expensive Hollywood spectacle is designed to reveal the world of the visible and the concrete rather than that of the unseen. Filming Christ's miracles risks transforming His story into a kind of science fiction. The Christ story, familiar to the point of *cliché*, is also more charged when its events are rendered symbolically rather than directly. Christ *figures* are likely to be more potent and complex dramatic characters than Christ Himself, just as symbolic crucifixions and resurrections can have more thematic impact than the literal Crucifixion and Resurrection of Christ.

Moses is an ideal film hero because his story is rich in visual possibilities and because he is himself a strong, simply drawn character defined by his external actions. From strapping Prince of Egypt to divinely chosen leader of his people, Moses is a more active and hence more usable dramatic character than Christ. Unlike Christ, Moses is not primarily a teacher or philosopher; and he is not a stoic. He is magician, prophet, lover, saviour, and unlike Jesus, he grows during the course of his story from ignorance to spiritual enlightenment, from worldly prince to holy man. Being human rather than divine, he is therefore more emotional, more malleable, than Christ; he is a passionate, wrathful, self-doubting prince. Charlton Heston's performance in DeMille's life of Moses has an elemental force and dignity. His massive physique, orotund voice, and granitic sobriety have true monumentality. His external performance, which matches DeMille's own methods, has surprising range and integrity.

The film presents Moses as a man of action seen most typically in long shot against a bustling panorama. A quintessential epic hero, Moses is a public figure who cannot afford too many personal problems. The epic hero, in general, does not have time for emotional complications, and it is noteworthy that Shakespeare's one full-fledged epic hero, Henry V, is also one of his least complex monarchs, a man presented almost exclusively in crowds. Henry is Shakespeare's most public character, an orator and political strategist who is defined by his ability to control the masses. In his film adaptation, Laurence Olivier further simplifies Shakespeare's king by removing passages that darken and complicate Henry's image. Olivier's Henry has none of the suggestions of tyranny and violence that are indicated in the play, and Olivier does not underline hints in the text that Henry is a cunning political operator and something of a poseur. Olivier's hero is an untarnished figure who has only one private moment in the film, when, on the night before the Battle of Agincourt, he muses on "ceremony" and the responsibilities of kingship. The film is even more pageantlike and nationalistic than the play, having been made to bolster English morale during wartime. It uses the epic mode to celebrate national victory and military glory, and even so Olivier's stentorian Henry, all bold surface and direct address, is one of the most vigorous and appealing epic heroes in films.

Another stirring epic hero, even less particularized than Henry, is Eisenstein's Alexander Nevsky, who has no character whatsoever apart from his heroic function. A determined policial saviour, he remains above personal interests; the film's feebly dramatised romantic triangle does not include him, for, like the most exalted of heroes, he is beyond sex. Nevsky's character is deliberately flattened because he is concerned exclusively with urgent matters of national defense. Like *Henry V*, the film was made as a warning to political enemies—its depiction of a Russian triumph in expelling marauding foreigners was intended to impress Hitler.

Nevsky is a pure hero of the sort rarely found in the Hollywood epic, where, too often, the political leader is allowed a romantic entanglement. For these single-minded heroes, however, romance is

The ideal epic hero: Laurence Olivier as Henry V.

seldom believable. Spartacus' affair with a slave girl only holds up the action; Moses's tryst with the Egyptian princess Nefertiti is an occasion for ludicrous soap opera dialogue; El Cid's passion for Celimene engenders the traditional neo-classic conflict between love and honor. Romance in the epic world is often intrusive because it detains the hero from achieving his destiny. Women are only in the way in the man's world of epic quests and challenges; like Penelope, they are best left to tending the hearth. Eisenstein's Nevsky is then unusual in remaining untouched by personal emotions. He has no identity apart from that of being a warrior engaged in the defence of his homeland; and because his heroism is rendered in physical rather than spiritual prowess, he is a splendid film hero.

The traditional epic hero in film is thus a generalised figure unmarred by personal eccentricity or psychological quirks. Obsessed by his destiny, his fate, his position as leader, he is not, however, presented as power-mad or as suffering from a saviour complex. His essential sanity and social integration are underscored by the presence in these roles of actors like Charlton Heston and Kirk Douglas. Heston, especially, seems incapable of playing a neurotic character. Though they express great feeling, wrath, and determination, Heston's

epic heroes exude physical and mental health. They are never remotely dangerous or insinuating, there is never the suggestion, as with Eisenstein's depiction of Ivan the Terrible, for instance, that the heroes may be deranged. Heston's string of larger-than-life characterisations (Moses, Ben-Hur, and El Cid are the most prominent) represents the apotheosis of American conservatism.

Occasionally, Hollywood epics have attempted to portray imperfect heroes. Unlike Heston's characters, who are themselves whole and who restore their society to moral and political order, these more complicated heroes accomplish awesome feats for wrong or ignoble reasons and destroy themselves in the process. Alexander the Great and Lawrence of Arabia are two such marred protagonists; and the films, which are generally acknowledged as literate

Two imperfect epic heroes: Richard Burton as Alexander the Great, 1956; Peter O'Toole as Lawrence of Arabia (with Anthony Quinn as an Arab chieftain).

106

epics, attempt to knock their heroes off the lofty heights occupied by the Heston characters. The choice of actors to portray these dark heroes is instructive, for neither Richard Burton (as Alexander) nor Peter O'Toole (as Lawrence) projects Heston's aura of absolute control. Burton and O'Toole have a sensual, hedonistic strain that presents a marked contrast to Heston's puritanism. Since they have a brash quality that thinly disguises deep wellsprings of self-pity and malaise, they are ideal choices for playing legendary egocentrics. Burton's Alexander and O'Toole's Lawrence are complex, contradictory characters.

Robert Rossen's screenplay turns Alexander into a modern neurotic who suffers from an acute Oedipal problem. The great conqueror is attached to and controlled by his dominating mother at the same time that he is locked in fierce competition with his warrior-father. The film provides Alexander with a thoroughly worked out family history, and so there is more of a domestic focus in this film than is customary for the *genre*. Rossen presents Alexander as a tyrant doomed to be dissatisfied because he wants more than the world has to offer him. The scenes of his mental disintegration, however, are blurred because Rossen flinches in his account of Alexander's sexual conflict. This 1956 film scrupulously avoids any suggestion of homosexuality, but Alexander's relationship to women is strangely detached. The character played by Claire Bloom wanders vaguely on the periphery of the action, demonstrating once again the secondary role of women and of romance in the epic *milieu*.

Rossen's concept of the conqueror as a self-destructive neurotic, and especially his account of Alexander's decline and early death at thirty-two, are ambiguous. Still, his film represents a rare attempt to probe beneath the stereotyped heroics of a legendary historical character, and Burton's expansive, ranting performance, bearing the stamp of a classically trained stage actor, is impressive.

Peter O'Toole's Lawrence, aided by Robert Bolt's intelligent screenplay and by David Lean's masterful direction, is surely close to the difinitive epic hero in films. Yet, unlike most epic heroes, Lawrence is seriously flawed, confined by consuming ambivalent relationships with the primitive Arab culture he risks his life to save and with the imperialistic British government he represents. Sceptic, idealist, introspective man of action, Lawrence was haunted by contradictions. A deeply private man, he yet sought, indeed required, public prominence in a vast arena. Filled with self-loathing, he nonetheless saw himself from early childhood as a person chosen for some great endeavour. A romantic and a visionary, he was plagued by recurrent depression and by the feeling that all human activity is profitless. A great military figure, he was horrified by the savagery of war. An imperialist, he was a sharp critic of Britain's dissembling and self-serving attitude toward the Arabs. Most paradoxical of all, Lawrence, after having led an oppressed people out of bondage, after having taken it upon himself to rearrange history, withdrew from public affairs, renounced his celebrity, and joined the ranks of the RAF. For the last two decades of his life, he worked in deliberate obscurity, bedevilled by that phantom of his own devising, the questing knight Lawrence of Arabia. He lived like a wounded Conrad hero by restricting his field of activity, devoting himself single-mindedly to the small tasks at hand. It was a desperately cramped existance, and one that Lawrence, now called Ross, needed in order to erase his fame.

The most self-conscious of modern heroes, he conspired in the creation of his own legend as a man of mystery. In *The Seven Pillars of Wisdom*, he placed his fabled neuroses on public display. And yet, for all the explorations into his coiled psychology, by Lawrence himself as well as by his several biographers, he has remained an elusive, shadowy figure, a man driven by demons only partially understood. David Lean's splendid film presents an unfinished portrait that only hints at the man's tortured homosexuality and its connection to his heroic role in the Arab Revolt. The film suggests, glancingly, that there is a connection between the character's will for self-punishment and his homosexuality. Lawrence relishes violence, and the most striking image in the film is the close-up of him spattered with blood, after he has superintended the slaughter of an enemy village, and weeping uncontrollably. A self-styled martyr, Lawrence makes a tantalising epic hero, and if the screenplay offers only a partial interpretation of his background and motivations, it does so with great intelligence.

The advertisements for the film showed Lawrence half-masked by darkness, and the image suited the picture's tolerance for ambiguity. Like many other epic heroes, Lawrence is a mystic and therefore ultimately unknowable. His deep mysteriousness is in fact part of the fabric of his greatness, and

Gregory Peck as Ahab, the supremely neurotic epic hero, in John Huston's Moby Dick, *1956.*

Lawrence of Arabia is one of the few epic films in which the hero's tortured psychology lends him legendary stature. Lawrence's neurotic maladjustments and his shifting attitudes to heroism, powerfully realised in Peter O'Toole's immense performance, assert his moral grandeur.

An even more twisted non-conformist epic hero than Lawrence is Melville's Captain Ahab in *Moby Dick*. Unlike Lawrence, though, Ahab's goals are private rather than social; Ahab is obsessed with a personal quest, and his compulsive search for the white whale has none of the political overtones that are customary for epic subjects. Since, however, his obsessions are externalised, Ahab is a potential film hero despite his interiority. But the casting of Gregory Peck in John Huston's 1956 film version sadly reduces Melville's great tortured hero to a species of middle-class adventurer with some minor

tics. Peck tries, but he is hopelessly sane and well-adjusted, and Huston's handsome, anaemic production never for a moment approaches Melville's exhilarating epic canvas.

A secondary class of epic hero is not a saviour but is himself saved after having been tested by a series of reversals and challenges. Ben-Hur, Barabbas, and the heroes of stories built on the pattern of *Quo Vadis?* and *The Sign of the Cross*, are all transformed by Chrisitanity. Characters like Natasha in *War and Peace*, Scarlett O'Hara, the orphans of the storm, and Dr. Zhivago, become heroic by surviving cataclysmic social and political upheaval. Whether through their experience with religion or war, these secondary heroic prototypes are greatly strengthened. Stories in which characters are transformed by tumultuous experience have a direct emotional appeal and often have a melodramatic rather than tragic base. None of the heroes of this type changes the world, each instead having been transfigured by world-shattering events like the Crucifixion, the French Revolution, the Civil War, and the Russian Revolution. Under the pressure of extreme circumstances which entirely disrupt their lives, the characters undergo a momentous emotional conversion, and their capacity to survive, and to mature, is the measure of their heroism. These characters naturally lack the stature of history-makers like Moses and Alexander and Lawrence; but they attain a different kind of heroism with which popular audiences can more readily identify.

Characters like Barabbas—an archetypal sufferer—achieve heroic dimension through their endurance. A common thief, chosen by the populace to be freed instead of Christ, Barabbas is the original infidel. Through a series of misfortunes—twenty years underground working in the mines, and then confinement in a gladiatorial school—he moves closer to the spirit of Christ. It is a common assumption in Hollywood's Christian epics that those characters whose lives touch Christ's, even if only for a privileged moment, are spiritually transformed. Dim-witted Barabbas needs a long time to discern the change in him; others see it before he does, and he acquires a reputation in the mines both as the man for whom Christ died and as a man with special capacities to endure hardship. He becomes a kind of *shaman*, indestructible and, in his own primitive way, wise. He is tortured by his memories of the Crucifixion, and it takes him many years to climb out of the pit of darkness. At the end of his journey, though he has not known where he was going, he finds his life by embracing Christian martyrdom. Hanging Christ-like on a cross, he has at last been purified.

Significantly, our first view of Barabbas is in a dungeon, encircled by darkness; our last view of him is on a cross—his journey describes a symbolic progression from darkness to illumination. Anthony Quinn's strong performance captures both Barabbas's brutish qualities as well as his evolving wisdom.

The heroes of *Quo Vadis?, The Sign of the Cross,* and *The Robe* follow a similar pattern of conversion and transcendence. The movement of these heroes from pagan scepticism to Christian piety is enacted in worldly terms. The three characters are acclaimed soldiers who embody the martial spirit of pagan Rome and who begin to change only when

they fall in love with nubile Christian maidens. The reluctant Roman soldiers are representative characters confronted with a grave and simple moral choice between heresy and faith. Their challenge is dramatised in broad and accessible terms—they are average people whos values are shaken by powerful events. It is by design that the Roman soldiers as played by Robert Taylor in *Quo Vadis?* and Fredric March in *The Sign of the Cross* are utterly bland; they're Everymen without any individuality whatsoever. Richard Burton's agonised Roman in *The Robe* is a happy departure from the tradition of the stoic soldier hero in Chrisitan epics. Burton challenges the movie tradition of playing the Roman sceptic as a robot, and he presents his character as a man tormented by an awesome power, whose conversion is a coiled and dangerous undertaking. Whereas Taylor and March attempt merely to absorb grandeur from the swirling backgrounds and spectacular production values, and are therefore bogus heroes, Burton tries to pitch his performance on a genuinely heroic scale.

Similar to the struggling heroes of Christian epics are the character types—again Barabbas is a prototype—who achieve heroic stature not through controlling their environment, like Sparacus or Alexander or Nevsky, but through being victimised by it. They are heroic by virtue of the scale and the consequences of their suffering. Not surprisingly, this kind of heroism-through-suffering is often enacted by women: Griffith's orphans of the storm, Tolstoy's Natasha, or by an essentially passive hero like Dr. Zhivago who reacts *to* events rather than creating them. Natasha is the best representative of this epic mode, since the experience of war changes her from a spoiled childlike girl to a wise young woman. In King Vidor's splendidly visual but superficial version of Tolstoy's novel, Audrey Hepburn skilfully portrays the stages of Natasha's development: foolish and selfish at first, she matures by living through the disruptions of war and of romantic disappointment. As is customary for epics, the rise and fall of her private life reflects the national fortunes.

The kind of epic that has a passive central character and that is propelled by a series of catastrophes receives its most sentimental treatment in *Orphans of the Storm*. The fate of the orphans— sisters who are separated and engulfed by a society in the throes of the French Revolution—is milked shamelessly for pathos; but it is an indication of

Heroism through suffering: Audrey Hepburn as Natasha, in King Vidor's War and Peace, 1956; *the Gish Sisters, in* Orphans of the Storm.

Griffith's power that this fundamentally bathetic story attains the dignity and spaciousness that are epic prerequisites. Lillian Gish's intense performance transforms the saccharine material. The famous scene in which she is reunited with her blind sister has the emotional grandeur of recognition scenes in classical drama. The film, like other historical essays by Griffith, offers a parochial and simplistic view of its subject, yet it is a powerful depiction of the impact of war on innocent characters, and it gives audiences the sense of living through a full emotional experience with the sisters. Like Dreyer's *Passion of Joan of Arc*, Griffith's movie achieves magnitude through the ecstatic suffering of its heroines: the women deepen the film-maker's canvas. Dreyer's *Passion* is probably the greatest interior epic in films, but Griffith's *Orphans of the Storm*, though conceived in a more expansive and romantic mode, attains an equivalent emotional heightening through the Gish sisters' exalted performances, the apotheosis of silent film technique.

The most famous epic sufferer in movies is Ben-Hur. The 1925 version, directed by Fred Niblo, with Ramon Novarro, and the 1959 William Wyler version, with Charlton Heston, are in many ways high points of the Hollywood epic for their respective periods. Ben-Hur, however, is not a traditional epic hero since he leads no armies, conquers no foreign lands, effects no sweeping changes in his society. Ben-Hur is neither a conqueror nor a saviour, neither a messiah nor a wise man capable of influencing millions, and yet he is probably the most popular of epic heroes in American films. General Lew Wallace's immensely popular Christian potboiler links a mostly fictional hero to the story of Christ, thereby gaining for Ben-Hur's adventures a kind of artificial high seriousness. Portentously subtitled *A Tale of the Christ*, the film aggressively seeks to elevate itself by criss-crossing its hero's labyrinthine journey with the Passion of Christ. The film opens with the birth of Christ; the hero receives water from Christ as he is on his way to serving time as a galley slave; he attends the Sermon on the Mount, and stands by at Calvary and the Crucifixion. Ben-Hur's own story, which traces the conventional melodramatic curve of eminence, fall, and recovery, is thus framed by the presence of the Holy One. The hero's confrontations with Christ are presented as privileged moments, as certificates of the film's momentousness.

Ben-Hur, then, like Barabbas and the generic *Quo Vadis?* hero, is an important character because, symbolically, he is Everyman saved by Christ. His story of misfortune and ultimate salvation is a reflection of Christ's own agony and transcendence. Unlike Barabbas, Ben-Hur does not give up his life. Christ's death frees him, and he is reunited with his mother, his sister, and his best girl. As in *The Robe*, Christ's death and Resurrection are accompanied by a cosmic upheaval—a torrential downpour destroys the old way and cleanses the land in preparation for the new life.

The attempt to gain prestige for the hero by this extracurricular pattern of associations with the ultimate Hero is of course a gimmick—yet it works. Ben-Hur's adventures, replete with spectacle, high emotion, and an emphatic theme, comprise the elements of a quintessential film epic.

Experience does not fundamentally change Ben-Hur so much as it reinforces traits already present from the beginning. Unlike other kinds of epic heroes, Ben-Hur does not grow to nobility through the pressure of external or internal conflicts; he is quite grand in the first place, being a prince of his people, a model son, a loyalist and privileged member of his community. His quarrel with his childhood friend Messala, who has become a fierce Roman, and the subsequent calamities—the break-up of his family, the loss of his money, servitude as a galley slave, adoption by a Roman senator, the chance to avenge his enemy in the chariot race—only confirm his strength of character. He is a paradigm of manliness, yet he is a hugely likable character because he is not saintly. He lusts for revenge against Messala; as if obeying the Old Testament rather than the New, he avidly seeks an eye for an eye.

Also unlike the heroes of traditional epics, Ben-Hur's goals are limited and personal; he seeks no more than revenge against his boyhood friend, and reunion with his mother and sister and *fiancée*. Yet, on film, he is a glorious epic hero. His experiences, with the high points of the naval battle in Part One and the chariot race in Part Two, have a visual impact that can be fully realised only on film. Ben-Hur isn't a remote, larger-than-life figure like Alexander or Henry V, but a superior mortal man who is severely tried and who triumphs at the last, saved not only by Christ but by his own strength as well. It is the achievement of both versions of Ben-Hur that when he is reunited at the end with his three women, we feel we have been through a stirring and significant experience with him. For all their contrivance and their *kitsch*-like qualities, the films achieve a sense of purgation that is essential to the experience of the epic mode as well as the tragic.

Charlton Heston as Ben-Hur, Hollywood's quintessential epic hero.

8. High Adventures, Swashbucklers, and Other Non-Epics

The Epic That Never Was (1973) is a compilation of interviews with people who worked on Josef von Sternberg's unfinished film of *I, Claudius*. Many large-scale films that *were* completed might also qualify as unfinished epics. Sometimes, the films miss epic stature because they attach the trappings of epic style to a story and characters that cannot support them. Sometimes, the films trivialise potential epic material. Among the most representative failed epics, films in which form and content are unevenly matched, are *Duel in the Sun, The Big Country, Ryan's Daughter* (1971) and *Barry Lyndon* (1975). Significantly, the films were all made by directors who have proven their skill in the epic *genre*. *Duel in the Sun* was produced by David O. Selznick as a follow-up to *Gone with the Wind* (itself an unsatisfactory epic, though a rousing romantic melodrama), and directed by King Vidor, who had established his reputation with lavish productions like *The Big Parade* (1925) and who ended his career in the Fifties with *War and Peace* and *Solomon and Sheba*. The year after he made *The Big Country*, William Wyler directed *Ben-Hur,* one of the most accomplished of Hollywood epics. David Lean's *Ryan's Daughter* has the expansive style the director had developed successfully in both *Lawrence of Arabia* and *Dr. Zhivago;* and Stanley Kubrick gave *Barry Lyndon* the visual amplitude that had served him so well on earlier projects like *Spartacus* and *2001*. Yet these failed epics are, in fact, victims of their directors' attraction to size and splendour. All four films have slender narratives and thinly developed characterisations that are suffocated by the spectacular visual embellishments. In each film, the monumental technique is easily detachable from the story, and so the films can be appreciated only as a display of bravura craftsmanship.

Duel in the Sun is an inordinately lavish western whose story is altogether undeserving of the grand style. The film has a portentous prologue spoken in hushed reverence by Orson Welles at his most mellifluous. This narrative introduction strains to lend mythic stature to the story of Pearl Chavez and her doomed love affair by enshrining her burial place as a kind of holy ground. The vivid sunsets, the stunning long shots of the parched Southwestern landscape, all conspire to impart the aura of legend to the shabby events that follow. The overstated opening is typical of the film's emphatic methods.

Claude Rains and Vivien Leigh, in Caesar and Cleopatra, *1945. Gabriel Pascal gave the film all the elaborate trappings of the Hollywood epic and thereby destroyed the tone of Shaw's sly, small-scale, anti-heroic comedy.*

Pearl's story begins as the camera swirls into one of the most cavernous saloons in films, its dimensions approaching those of the Roman Forum, and it closes with a shoot-out between the ill-fated lovers filmed against lurid sunsets.

The film has all the signposts of the grandiose Hollywood epic: extreme long shots of the vast landscape, a picturesque, isolated mansion, a spectacular party scene, a confrontation between railroad barons and farmers that is treated as if it were of decisive historical consequence. But the oversized gestures are merely trappings without substance—a display of elephantine production values inappropriately bestowed on a puny story of purely private focus. Pearl Chavez, the tempestuous half-breed, makes an unconvincing epic heroine because her passions are not connected to a larger historical or social context. King Vidor's energetic direction and

Selznick's all-out production cannot conceal the fact that the story is merely a series of elaborate set pieces in search of a theme.

In *The Big Country*, another overblown formula western, William Wyler uses the wide screen with splendid assurance. More audacious here than in the ultra-respectable *Ben-Hur*, he revels in extreme long shots in which the characters are dwarfed by the rugged western terrain. Wyler delights in sharp juxtapositions between long shots and close-ups, and his camerawork is probably more fluent and mobile than in any other wide screen film of the Fifties. Uninhibited by the dimensions of the CinemaScope screen, Wyler avoids the static, sedate quality that disfigured many of the films of the period. *The Big Country* dramatises the climactic shoot-out between rival landowners in a series of stunning, exaggerated long shots. The virtuoso camera set-ups and the pulsing, driving music conspire to convince us that the shabby story has epic thrust. Because the visual magnificence and the threadbare plot are so clearly at odds, however, the film is reduced to being a delirious stylistic exercise. When, in *Ben-Hur*, Wyler had material with genuine epic dimension, he held himself in, adopting a more sober approach that has little of the sense of freewheeling experimentation with the large screen that distinguishes *The Big Country*.

Ryan's Daughter, a modest story about an extramarital affair set vaguely against the background of the Irish Revolution, has none of the urgency or excitement of *Lawrence of Arabia* or *Dr. Zhivago*; and yet Lean gives it the lush painterly style he had perfected for the two earlier blockbusters. The characters' emotions are given cosmic significance, so that their feelings influence the weather and transform the landscape. As always in Lean's films, the natural world is spectacularly rendered— towering cliffs, sylvan forests, a churning ocean,

idyllic sand dunes, a quaint town nestled in a lush countryside. As Pauline Kael has written, the film gives a face-lift to the world. But the visual enhancement is too strong for the simple story and plain characters. The film is really a sentimental romance, intimate in focus, that needs the simplicity of the early Lean of *Brief Encounter* rather than the epic mannerisms of the later films.

Barry Lyndon is the ultimate coffee-table movie. The Eighteenth-century world is evoked with loving, authentic detail, each shot composed with painstaking solemnity. The castles, the formal gardens, the glowing interiors, the battles, the balls, the exquisitely embroidered costumes, are all breathtaking, and the elegantly poised images are heightened by the often elegiac music. The deliberate, stately pacing, the carefully posed actors, the de la Tour lighting, give the film the formal precision of a

Jennifer Jones and Gregory Peck in the lavish party scene, in King Vidor's Duel in the Sun, *1946, a preposterously inflated Western that seems almost like a parody of the conventions of the Hollywood epic.*

115

Charles Bickford oversees the roundup of his enemies in another overblown Western, William Wyler's The Big Country, *1958.*

In Dr. Zhivago, *1965, David Lean's monumental Moscow street scene serves his vast historical narrative. The same expansive style, however, was excessive for the intimate love story of* Ryan's Daughter, *1971. In the scene here, Christopher Jones and Sarah Miles have an ecstatic reunion on a hill overlooking the ocean.*

Ryan O'Neal as the hero, in Stanley Kubrick's meaninglessly elegant Barry Lyndon, *1975.*

religious ritual. Yet the decorum is lavished inappropriately on a picaresque tale of a rogue's circular progress from penury to fortune to penury. The hero is a featherweight whose history reveals no significant social, or political, or moral insights, and since Kubrick's controlled direction relegates him to being a stick figure in a busy tapestry, he remains practically invisible; the character of Barry Lyndon himself is inessential to the effects that Kubrick is trying to create. Thus freed from involvement with the characters, we can savour the meticulous reconstruction of a historical period; we are invited to linger over the film's luxurious surfaces. *Barry Lyndon* is a celebration of its own consummate elegance.

Kubrick has presented the material as if it had the cosmic reverberations of *2001*, yet the film has almost no theme whatsoever. In effect, it is an abstract film, as cold and precise and grand as *2001*, but where style is inseparable from content in that film, manner is rigorously separated from matter in *Barry Lyndon*. The story is merely a pretext for the director to display his virtuosity, whereas in *2001* the monumentality evolved organically from the theme. The automaton acting, the long takes and sedentary camera, the sonorous music, were a

natural extension of the futuristic world the film presents; here, the glacial tone is there for its own sake, as an expression of the director's infatuation with a certain kind of depersonalised, icily glittering world view.

These four unsuccessful films all provide fascinating glimpses of epic topography. The films are disconnected in odd and interesting ways from the stories they tell; and because they use film to express the director's personal interest in style, they are respectable failures.

Whole classes of Hollywood spectacles lack epic magnitude because their tone is lightweight. Swashbucklers, costume romances, high adventure dramas don't aspire to epic status, deliberately downplaying epic qualities that may be part of their material. Films like *Ivanhoe* (1952), *The Knights of the Round Table* (1954), *Quentin Durward* (1955), *The Three Musketeers* (1948), *Scaramouche* (1951), *The Prisoner of Zenda* (1951), *The Thief of Bagdad*, *Robin Hood* (1922 and 1938), *Prince Valiant* (1954), *The Black Shield of Falworth* (1955), and *The Guns of Navarone* (1961) aim to be lighthearted and agreeable, and avoid the essential seriousness of purpose that defines the epic mode. These films are the quivalent of ballads and romances in literature. Their stories about heroes have a more limited focus than epics and have a brighter, crisper tone. Ballads and romances are meant primarily to entertain and only secondarily to underline a moral or to reveal some historical insight. Romances do not have the weight of religious and national themes that concern the epic storyteller, though these themes may be part of the fabric of the romance, in a muted way. The plots of romance are usually more complicated, and have more digressions, than the typical epic narrative, which may begin *in media re* but which usually adheres to a fairly tight narrative development. The hero of romance has more time for women than the epic hero; trained in a courtly tradition, he regards his comportment as a lover as an essential part of his manly code. The hero of romance, bred in the rules of chivalry, is more likely than the epic hero to prove himself in combat, to test and to purify himself, for the sake of his lady.

Comedy rather than tragedy is the dominant tone in the swashbuckler romances. The dashing athletic hero is not, like the epic hero, chosen by fate to defend his people. There is little sense of historical necessity or of national destiny in the swashbuckler. These lighthearted films stress swordplay and agility—the physical moment is of primary interest, and this makes the material especially suitable for movies.

The heroes of adventure and romance often face the same kind of experiences as the epic hero. They often rescue their country from evil government, and so their derring-do is enacted against matters of national concern. And they all undergo some kind of conversion: they are tested, and they pass. At first

Robert Taylor as a lacklustre Ivanhoe, 1952. Swashbuckling heroes like Ivanhoe belong to the fictional world of romance rather than epic.

vagabonds and wastrels, gaily uncommitted, seemingly irresponsible, they are forced through the pressures of exceptional challenges to discover and to use their leadership abilities. Ivanhoe and Robin Hood save England from the mismanagement of the evil Prince John in order to return the country to the beloved absent King, Richard the Lion-Heart. The Thief of Bagdad saves his city from foreign aggressors. Prince Valiant, like the youngest of the musketeers, engages in a series of adventures by means of which the untried boy from the provinces is turned into a man.

The actors chosen to portray swashbuckling heroes—Douglas Fairbanks, Errol Flynn, Robert Taylor, Ronald Colman, Robert Wagner, Tony Curtis—are lightweight matinee idols. With their flashing smiles, their remarkable agility, their captivating insouciance, Fairbanks and Flynn are Hollywood's greatest swashbucklers. They have the unmistakable aura of playboys, and nothing so solemn as an epic theme is allowed to intrude into the fantasy world their films set up and jealously guard. Fairbanks and Flynn are gay blades who have an ironic detachment from the adventures they glide through so gracefully. Nobility, earnestness, steadfastness of purpose, are foreign notions to them. Robert Taylor and Tony Curtis, the reigning swordsmen of the early Fifties, lack their predecessors' wit and flair, and their costume films are therefore much less entertaining than those of the original swashbucklers. In *Ivanhoe* and *The Knights of the Round Table*, Robert Taylor is a dull, modern-seeming knight; and the films appear to have been scaled downward to accommodate him. Directed by Metro-Goldwyn-Mayer's in-house man for costume pictures, Richard Thorpe, these Fifties stories of medieval knights lack the exuberance, the dash and verve, of the earlier Fairbanks and Flynn opuses. The depiction of the past in the Fifties' romances is colourless, though often academically correct. The sets and costumes, the jousts and hand-to-hand combats, are well managed; the editing in the scenes of fighting is invariably crisp. But the films, lacking a point of view about the past, have a mechanical, assembly-line quality.

Medieval romance has never been rendered imaginatively or creatively in an American film, though the dark religious medieval sensibility has been evoked powerfully in European films like Lang's *Siegfried*, Dreyer's *Passion of Joan of Arc*, Bergman's *The Seventh Seal*, and Bresson's *Lance-*

lot du Lac. The finest re-creation of the Middle Ages in American movies is probably Fairbanks's *Robin Hood,* in which William Cameron Menzies's cavernous sets, with their thrusting arches and receding hallways, have a simple grandeur that befits the period.

Swashbucklers, then, deliberately lack the weight and scope of epics, and the glamorous swashbuckling hero is even more externally presented than the epic hero. The swashbuckler is always and readily a man of action who seems to have no interior; and the natural propensity of films for capturing externals makes this kind of hero ideal for the medium. On their own terms, Fairbanks's and Flynn's high adventures are wonderfully engaging; their films wink at the audience, they have a sly sense of put-on, of burlesque. Richard Lester's recent musketeer films (*The Three Musketeers,* 1973;

The Four Musketeers, 1974) were redundant because they were parodies of parodies, mocking material which had never been taken seriously in the first place. Their satiric thrusts were aimed at limp and inappropriate targets.

Fairbanks's *The Thief of Bagdad* is the most vivacious swashbuckler in American movies. Its witty, soaring, stylised sets (by Menzies) are almost as grand as Griffith's Babylon, but for all their stupendous scale, they are lightweight in their effect rather than massive; airy and fanciful and therefore well-matched to the star's own personality. One touch of heaviness in the sets and the movie's frolicsome tone is threatened. The film maintains a consistent exuberance that is invigorating.

Swashbucklers, romances, high adventures, ballads of love and honour, are not epics. When they know their place, though, and are certain of their

Oliver Reed, Michael York, Richard Chamberlain, and Frank Finlay, in Richard Lester's parody of a parody, The Three Musketeers, *1974.*

120

The most captivating swashbuckler in American movies: Douglas Fairbanks, in The Thief of Bagdad, *1924.*

tone, they are not so much poor relatives to the epic as likable additions to the spectacle canon.

Hollywood rarely makes legitimate epics anymore. The lavish spectacle movie has passed out of favour, a victim of a tightened economy and declining audience interest. The tradition-bound epic movie is already something of a historical relic. Like the pictures themselves, the great, gaudy movie palaces that were built (in the Teens, Twenties, and early Thirties) to display the big films, are also an index of the taste and sensibility of an earlier period. The baroque splendour of the mammoth movie palaces was the perfect setting for the "colossal" film. The cavernous, aggressively ornate interiors of these gilt-encrusted theatres often in fact looked like the sets in a DeMille movie, their *décor* being strictly Southern California interpretations of Oriental and Mediterranean *motifs*.

The theatres, located in deteriorating inner cities, are becoming rarities. Many of the palaces have been torn down to make room for skyscrapers or parking lots, and most of the remaining theatres (if they are open at all, and not just standing there in mute desolation) have long since lost their glamorous, exclusive first-run status. They are seemingly condemned to showing kung fu and black exploitation thrillers, their balconies closed off, their huge orchestra sections sparsely attended by patrons totally indifferent to their spectacular surroundings. The theatres are simply too big and too fancy (too overpowering and even a little ominous) for modern streamline taste.

The glitter of the movie palaces began to fade in the early Sixties, about the time that Hollywood's second epic phase started to lose momentum; and the final glory for many of the theatres were their reserved-seat, advanced-price engagements of films like *Ben-Hur, King of Kings, Spartacus, Exodus,* and *The Greatest Story Ever Told*.

In their heyday, the way epic films were presented to the public was often as elaborate as the films themselves. The big movies were accorded lengthy, reserved-seat engagements in huge theatres all spruced up for the occasion; the price scale, the two-a-day performance schedule, the intermission interval, and the spectacular poster and marquee displays in front of the theatre were all designed to impress the filmgoer with the dignity and prestige of the motion picture event. That kind of showmanship no longer attracts audiences. The last reserved-seat movie in America was *Last Tango in Paris*, which received the special treatment not because it was a four-hour, multimillion dollar cast of thousands mightiest-spectacle-ever epic but because it was a sexual curiosity.

They don't make reserved-seat epics any more because it would cost too much to make the films in high style and because there is not a sufficient audience to guarantee a profit. Like the dismantled or empty or aging Orpheums, Palaces, Orientals, States, Paramounts, Albees, and Foxes, the epic is a reminder, a historical artifact, of a great, splashy, madcap Hollywood that was.

Selected Bibliography

Auerbach, Erich. *Mimesis. The Representation of Reality in Western Literature*. (New York: Doubleday Anchor, 1957.)

Barna, Yon. *Eisenstein. The Growth of a Cinematic Genius*. (Boston: Little, Brown; London: Secker and Warburg, 1973.)

Barr, Charles. "Cinemascope: Before and After," in *Film Quarterly*, vol. 16, number 4, 1963.

Bazin, André. *What is Cinema?* Vols. 1 and 2, edited and translated by Hugh Gray. (Berkeley: University of California, 1967.)

Bitzer, Billy. *The Autobiography of D. W. Griffith's Master Cameraman*. (New York: Farrar, Straus and Giroux, 1973.)

Carpenter, Rhys. *Folk Tale, Fiction, and Saga in the Homeric Epics*. (Berkeley: University of California Press, 1946.)

Cary, John. *Spectacular. The Story of Epic Films*. (New York: Castle Books, 1974.)

Chase, Mary Ellen. *The Bible and the Common Reader*. (New York: Macmillan, 1945.)

Clay, Albert T. *The Origin of Biblical Traditions*. (New Haven: Yale University Press, 1923.)

Cook, Albert Spaulding. *The Classic Line. A Study in Epic Poetry*. (Bloomington: Indiana University Press, 1966.)

Eisenstein, Sergei. *Film Form*, (New York: Harcourt Brace Jovanovich, 1949.)

———. *Film Sense*. (New York: Harcourt Brace Jovanovich, 1942.)

Eisner, Lotte H. *The Haunted Screen*. (Berkeley: University of California Press; London: Secker and Warburg, 1973.)

Essoe, Gabe, and Raymond Lee. *DeMille: The Man and His Pictures*. (New Jersey: A. S. Barnes & Co., 1970.)

Foerster, Donald Madison. *The Fortunes of Epic Poetry. A Study in English and American Criticism, 1750-1950*. (Washington, D. C.: The Catholic University of America Press, 1962.)

Gardiner, John H. *The Bible as English Literature*. (New York: Scribner's, 1918.)

Geduld, Carolyn. *Film Guide to 2001: A Space Odyssey*. (Bloomington: Indiana University Press, 1973.)

Greene, Thomas M. *The Descent from Heaven. A Study in Epic Continuity*. (New Haven: Yale University Press, 1963.)

Gunkel, Hermann. *The Legends of Genesis. The Biblical Saga and History*. (New York: Schocken, 1964.)

Hart, Walter Morris. *Ballad and Epic. A Study in the Development of the Narrative Art*. (New York: Russell and Russell, 1967.)

Henderson, Robert M. *D. W. Griffith. The Years at Biograph*. (New York: Farrar, Straus and Giroux; London: Secker and Warburg, 1970.)

———. *D. W. Griffith*. (New York: Oxford University Press, 1972.)

Jacobs, Lewis. *The Rise of the American Film*. (New York: Teachers College Press, 1939, and reissued 1968.)

Jarratt, Vernon. *The Italian Cinema*. (London: The Falcon Press, 1951.)

Ker, William Paton. *Epic and Romance; Essays on Medieval Literature*. (London: Macmillan, 1926.)

Kirk, G. S. *The Songs of Homer*. (Cambridge: Harvard University Press, 1962.)

Kracauer, Siegfried. *From Caligari to Hitler: A Psychological History of the German Film*. (Princeton, New Jersey: Princeton University Press, 1947.)

Lang, Andrew. *Homer and the Epic*. (London: Longmans, Green, & Co., 1893.)

Leprohon, Pierre. *The Italian Cinema*. (New York: Praeger; London: Secker and Warburg, 1972.)

Lord, Albert Bates. *The Singer of Tales*. (Cambridge: Harvard University Press, 1960.)

Merchant, Paul. *The Epic*. (London: Methuen, 1971.)

Moorman, Charles. *A Knyght There was. The Evolution of the Knight in Literature*. (Lexington: The University of Kentucky Press, 1961.)

Murray, Gilbert. *The Rise of the Greek Epic*. (London: Oxford University Press, 1934.)

O'Dell, Paul. *Griffith and the Rise of Hollywood*. (New Jersey: A. S. Barnes & Co.; London: The Tantivy Press, 1970.)

Ramsaye, Terry. *A Million and One Nights. A History of the Motion Picture Through 1925*. (New York: Simon & Schuster, 1926.)

Schrader, Paul. *Transcendental Style in Film*. (Berkeley: University of California Press, 1972.)

Silva, Fred, ed. *Focus on The Birth of a Nation*. (New Jersey: Prentice-Hall, 1971.)

Stack, Oswald. *Pasolini*. (Bloomington: Indiana University Press; London: Secker and Warburg, 1970.)

Tillyard, E. M. W. *The English Epic and its Background*. (New York: Oxford University Press, 1954.)

———. *The Epic Strain in the English Novel*. (London: Chatto and Windus, 1958.)

Vardac, A. Nicholas. *Stage to Screen. Theatrical Method from Garrick to Griffith*. (New York: Benjamin Blom, 1968.)

Warshow, Robert. "The Gangster as Tragic Hero" and "Movie Chronicle: The Westerner," in *The Immediate Experience*. (New York: Atheneum, 1972.)

Watts, Ann Chalmers. *The Lyre and the Harp. A Comparative Reconsideration of Oral Tradition in Homer and Old English Epic Poetry*. (New Haven: Yale University Press, 1969.)

Whitman, Cedric Hubbell. *Homer and the Heroic Tradition*. (Cambridge: Harvard University Press, 1958.)

Wilkie, Brian. *Romantic Poets and Epic Tradition*. (Madison: University of Wisconsin Press, 1965.)

Wilson, Edmund. " 'You Can't Do This to Me! ' Shrilled Celia," in *Classics and Commercials*. (New York: Vintage, 1962.)

Wood, Michael. *America in the Movies*. (New York: Basic Books; London: Secker and Warburg, 1975.)

Selected Filmography

The Adventures of Robin Hood. Warner Bros. 1938. Dir. Michael Curtiz. Scr. Norman Reilly Raine, Seton I. Miller.

Alexander Nevsky. U.S.S.R. Mosfilm. 1938. Dir. Ser. S.M. Eisenstein.

Alexander the Great. United Artists. 1956. Dir./Scr. Robert Rossen.

America. United Artists. 1924. Dir. D.W. Griffith. Scr. John Pell.

Barabbas. Columbia. 1962. Dir. Richard Fleischer. Scr. Christopher Fry.

Battleship Potemkin. U.S.S.R. 1925. Dir. S.M. Eisenstein.

Ben-Hur. M-G-M. 1925. Dir. Fred Niblo. Scr. June Mathis, Carey Wilson, Bess Meredith.

Ben-Hur. M-G-M. 1959. Dr. William Wyler. Scr. Karl Tunberg.

The Bible. 20th Century-Fox. 1966. Dir. John Huston. Scr. Christopher Fry.

The Big Fisherman. Buena Vista. 1959. Dir. Frank Borzage. Scr. Howard Estabrook, Rowland Lee.

The Birth of a Nation. Epoch. 1915. Dir. D.W. Griffith. Scr. Griffith, Frank Woods.

The Buccaneer. Paramount 1938. Dir. Cecil B. DeMille. Edwin Justus Mayer, Harold Lamb.

The Buccaneer. Paramount. 1958. Dir. Anthony Quinn. Scr. Jesse L. Lasky Jr.

Cabiria. Italia Film. 1914. Dir. Giovanni Pastrone.

Ceasar and Cleopatra. Rank. 1945. Dir. Gabriel Pascal. Scr. George Bernard Shaw.

The Charge of the Light Brigade. Warner Bros. 1936. Dir. Michael Curtiz. Scr. Michael Jacoby, Rowland Leigh.

The Charge of the Light Brigade. United Artists. 1968. Dir. Tony Richardson. Scr. Charles Wood.

El Cid. Allied Artists. 1961. Dir. Anthony Mann. Philip Yordan.

Cimarron. RKO 1931. Dir. Wesley Ruggles. Scr. Howard Estabrook.

Cimarron. M-G-M. 1960. Dir. Anthony Mann. Scr. Arnold Schulman.

Civilization. Ince. 1916. Dir. Thomas H. Ince. Scr. C. Gardner Sullivan.

Cleopatra. Fox. 1917. Dir. J. Gordon Edwards.

Cleopatra. Paramount. 1934. Dir. Cecil B. DeMille. Scr. Waldemar Young, Barlett Comack.

Cleopatra. 20th Century-Fox. 1963. Dir. Joseph L. Mankiewicz. Scr. Mankiewicz, Ranald MacDougall, Sidney Buchman.

The Covered Wagon. Paramount. 1923. Dir. James Cruze. Scr. Jack Cunningham.

Crusades. Paramount. 1935. Dir. Cecil B. DeMille. Scr. Harold Lamb, Waldemar Young, Dudley Nichols.

David and Bathsheba. 20th-Fox. 1951. Dir. Henry King. Scr. Philip Dunne.

Demetrius and the Gladiators. 20th Century-Fox. 1954. Dir. Delmer Daves. Scr. Philip Dunne.

Doctor Zhivago. M-G-M. 1965. Dir. David Lean. Scr. Robert Bolt.

Duel in the Sun. Selznick. 1946. Dir. King Vidor. Scr. David O. Selznick.

The Egyptian. 20th Century-Fox. 1954. Dir. Michael Curtiz. Philip Dunne, Casey Robinson.

Esther and the King. 20th Century-Fox. 1960. Dir. Raoul Walsh. Scr. Walsh, Michael Elkins.

Exodus. United Artists. 1960. Dir. Otto Preminger. Scr. Dalton Trumbo.

The Fall of the Roman Empire. Bronston. 1964. Dir. Anthony Mann. Ben Barzman, Philip Yordan.

Fellini Satyricon. United Artists. 1969. Dir./Scr. Federico Fellini.

55 Days at Peking. Allied Artists. 1963. Dir. Nicholas Ray. Scr. Philip Yordan, Bernard Gordon.

Giant. Warner Bros. 1956. Dir. George Stevens. Scr. Fred Guoil, Ivan Moffatt.

Gone with the Wind. M-G-M. 1939. Dir. Victor Fleming. Scr. Sidney Howard.

The Greatest Story Ever Told. United Artists. 1965. Dir. George Stevens. Scr. James Lee Barrett, Stevens, Carl Sandburg.

Helen of Troy. Warner Bros. 1955. Dir. Robert Wise. Scr. Hugh Gray, John Twist.

Henry V. Rank. 1944. Dir. Laurence Olivier.

How the West Was Won. M-G-M. 1961. Dir. Henry Hathaway, John Ford, and George Marshall. Scr. James R. Webb.

Intolerance. Wark. 1916. Dir. D.W. Griffith.

Ivanhoe. M-G-M. 1952. Dir. Richard Thorpe. Scr. Noel Langley.

Ivan the Terrible. Part I and II. Mosfilm. 1943, 1946. Dir./Scr. S.M. Eisenstein.

Joan the Woman. Paramount. 1917. Dir. Cecil B. DeMille. Scr. Jeanie Macpherson.

John Paul Jones. Warner Bros. 1959. Dir. John Farrow. Scr. Farrow and Jesse Lasky, Jr.

Judith of Bethulia. Biograph. 1913. Dir. D.W. Griffith. Scr. Frank Woods.

King of Kings. PDC. 1927. Dir. Cecil B. DeMille. Scr. Jeanie Macpherson.

King of Kings. M-G-M. 1961. Dir. Nicholas Ray. Scr. Philip Yordan.

Knights of the Round Table. M-G-M. 1954. Dir. Richard Thorpe. Scr. Talbot Jennings, Noel Langley.

The Last Days of Pompeii. RKO. 1935. Dir. Ernest B. Schoedsack. Scr. Ruth Rose, Boris Ingster.

Lawrence of Arabia. Columbia. 1962. Dir. David Lean. Scr. Robert Bolt.

The Leopard. 20th Century-Fox. 1963. Dir. Luchino Visconti. Scr. Visconti, Suso Cecchi d'Amico.

The Longest Day. 20th Century-Fox. 1962. Dir. Ken Annakin, Andrew Marton, Bernard Wicki. Scr. Cornelius Ryan.

Metropolis. UFA. 1926. Dr. Fritz Lang. Scr. Thea von Harbou.

Napoleon. Société Générale de Film. 1927. Dir./Scr. Abel Gance.

The Nibelungen. UFA. 1924. (Part I: *Siegfried*. Part II: *Kriemhild's Revenge*) Dir. Fritz Lang. Scr. Thea von Harbou.

Nicholas and Alexandra. Columbia. 1971. Dir. Franklin Schaffner. Scr. James Goldman.

Noah's Ark. Warner Bros. 1928. Dir. Michael Curtiz. Scr. Anthony Coldaway.

Orphans of the Storm. United Artists. 1922. Dir. D.W. Griffith. Scr./Griffith.

Patton. 20th Century-Fox. 1969. Dir. Franklin Schaffner. Scr. Francis Ford Coppola.

Prince Valiant. 20th Century Fox. 1954. Dir. Henry Hathaway. Scr. Dudly Nichola.

The Prodigal. M-G-M. 1955. Dir. Richard Thorpe. Scr. Maurice Zimm.

Quo Vadis? M-G-M. 1951. Dir. Mervyn LeRoy. Scr. S.N. Behrman, John Lee Mahin.

The Robe. 20th Century-Fox. 1953. Dir. Henry Koster. Scr. Philip Dunne.

Robin Hood. United Artists. 1922. Dir. Allan Dwan. Scr. Douglas Fairbanks.

Salome. Columbia. 1953. Dir. William Dieterle. Scr. Harry Kleiner.

Samson and Delilah. Paramount. 1949. Dir. Cecil B. DeMille. Scr. Jesse L. Lasky, Frederic M. Frank.

San Francisco. M-G-M. 1936. Dir. W.S. Van Dyke. Scr. Anita Loos.

The Sign of the Cross. Paramount. 1932. Dir. Cecil B. DeMille. Waldemar Young, Sidney Buchman.

The Silver Chalice. Warner Bros. 1955. Dir. Victor Saville. Scr. Lesser Samuels.

Solomon and Sheba. United Artists. Dir. King Vidor. Scr. Anthony Veiller.

Spartacus. Universal International. 1960. Dir. Stanley Kubrick. Scr. Dalton Trumbo.

The Ten Commandments. Paramount. 1923. Dir. Cecil B. DeMille. Scr. Jeanie Macpherson.

The Ten Commandments. Paramount. 1956. Dir. Cecil B. DeMille. Scr. Aeneas MacKenzie, Jesse L. Lasky, Jr.

The Thief of Bagdad. United Artists. 1924. Dir. Raoul Walsh. Scr. Lotta Woods.

The Three Musketeers. 20th Century-Fox. 1973. Dir. Richard Lester. Scr. George MacDonald Fraser.

2001: A Space Odyssey. M-G-M. 1968. Dir. Stanley Kubrick. Scr. Kubrick, Arthur C. Clarke.

Ulysses. Paramount. 1953. Dir. Mario Camerini. Scr. Hugh Gray, Irvin Shaw, Ben Hecht, Ennio de Concini, Franco Brusati.

The Wanderer. Paramount. 1925. Dir. Raoul Walsh. Scr. James T. O'Donohue.

War and Peace. Paramount. 1956. Dir. King Vidor. Scr. Vidor, Bridget Boland, Mario Camerini, Ennio de Concini, Ivo Perilli.

War and Peace. Mosfilm. 1964-1967. Dir. Sergei Bondarchuk. Scr. Bondarchuk, Vasily Solovyov.

Waterloo. Columbia. 1970. Dir. Sergei Bondarchuk. Scr. Bondarchuk, H.A.L. Craig.

The Woman God Forgot. Paramount. 1917. Dir. Cecil B. DeMille. Scr. Jeanie Macpherson.

Index

Page numbers referring to illustrations are set in boldface.

DATE DUE	
APR 16 1998	
MAY 19 1998	

GAYLORD   PRINTED IN U.S.A.